HEARTACHES TO BLESSINGS

MEMOIR OF A BAKING CHAMP WHO REFUSED TO BE
KNOCKED DOWN AND OUT BY THE ROUGH
EXPERIENCES OF LIFE.

DIANE ROARK

Cover and interior designs: BeHoldings Publishing
Contributing Editor: Terry Toler, https://beholdings-publishing.myshopify.com/
For information or for booking email: dianeroark8484@gmail.com

First U.S. Edition: July, 2022
Printed in the United States of America
ISBN: 979-8-218-00742-3

Thank you for purchasing this memoir from best-selling author, Diane Roark. As an additional thank you, Diane would like to send you free gifts periodically.

If you'd like to receive:

Newsletters

Updates

New Releases

Announcements

Recipes

Sign up at:

https://wandering-butterfly-4036.ck.page/1d860b2617

Follow Diane at:

Facebook: https://www.facebook.com/recipesforourdailybread

Instagram: https://www.instagram.com/recipesforourbread/

Table of Contents

CHAPTER ONE

TODAY SHOW

A journey starts with one step.

"Congratulations! You won the dessert contest on the *TODAY Show*," the woman on the phone said to me. "We'll fly you to New York for an all-expense-paid trip to demonstrate your recipe live on-air. You're scheduled for Friday, May 19th."

I could feel my mouth gape open as I tried to understand. It took me a minute to realize I was talking to a producer from the *TODAY Show*, and she wanted me to demonstrate my recipe live in New York City. On live TV!

When I grasped the information, I felt nervous and excited at the same time. Excited to be a finalist because cooking was my passion, but nervous about going to New York, especially by myself. Big cities and the traffic that comes with them makes me uncomfortable. All my life, I've been directionally challenged and easily lost.

I was relieved when the producer said, 'We'll pick you up from the airport and take you to the hotel. It's a couple of blocks from Rockefeller Plaza and an easy walk to the studio."

Certainly, if it were an easy walk, I could find it, I thought.

But unfortunately, the date rang a bell. I couldn't make it. While I would love the opportunity to share my love of baking on the TODAY Show, family always comes first.

"I'm so excited, but I can't make it on Friday," I said. "My oldest daughter Carly is graduating from medical school. I can't miss it."

If only she'd said a different day. I couldn't help but feel a little sad. I was missing out on a once-in-a-lifetime chance to share my love of baking with such a large audience. When I was a teenager, I fell in love with baking and dreamed of owning a bakery. I baked desserts for my dad and siblings, who encouraged me to bake more. This love continued as I baked with and for all five of my children.

But Carly had worked so long and hard to become a medical doctor. I wasn't going to miss her special day. Her dream was to help children with medical problems, which came from witnessing all of my son Caleb's issues.

Caleb is a twin who was born breech with a terrible brain bleed. He has had seventeen brain surgeries, including shunt failure, plus infections including staph and pseudomonas twice in his brain. He also has cerebral palsy and seizures. He rarely speaks, but he understands what you tell him.

When Caleb was a toddler, I was determined to help him with his short-term memory loss. I'd sit him on the counter almost daily and we'd bake together. He eventually was able to memorize ingredients and amounts. Baking brought joy and healing to both of us. It also brought delight to our neighbors' faces when we shared our baked goods with them.

Needless to say, my plate was always full with the five kids, including, not only a special needs son, but two adopted children, and the sports, school, and church activities that came with the responsibilities of motherhood.

My dream of owning a bakery never happened.

When the producer told me they couldn't change the date, I repeated that I couldn't miss my daughter's graduation. As I was about to hang up, I placed the phone to my mouth again and said, "Can you have me home by five o'clock on Friday?"

"I promise you that we'll do everything we can to get you back home in time," she said.

My whole body tingled with joy. Maybe I could accomplish both on the same day. I said yes and decided to trust that God would get me safely to New York and back in time for Carly's big day.

Caleb's grin said it all when I told him I was a top-two finalist in the TODAY Show dessert contest. He was the one who had encouraged me to enter to begin with. One day, while watching the TODAY Show, he grabbed my arm and pulled me to the television. He didn't have to say a word, because I knew that he wanted me to enter the contest.

I did and the rest is history. It's amazing how God used Caleb to give me one of the biggest breaks of my career.

* * *

New York City

When I arrived in New York, my nerves eased as soon as I got off the plane and saw my driver waiting for me. I felt like a Food Network star with my private driver waiting to whisk me away.

He grabbed my bags, and we headed to the car. The timing was perfect as he had found a place to park along the curb.

The traffic was terrible, though. I asked the driver if he was used to it. He told me he'd lived there his whole life and knew how to handle those crazy drivers. I wasn't sure how anyone got used to it. Drivers were honking their horns, swerving in and out of lanes, slamming on brakes, and cutting in front of us.

I was out of my comfort zone, so I prayed, "Thank you, God, that I'm not driving. Please God, get me to the hotel safely."

The driver glanced at me several times in his mirror. He probably noticed the concern on my face. He may have seen me with my head down and praying.

"This is your first time in New York, isn't it?" he asked.

"Yes, sir," I said.

After learning I was from Little Rock, he asked if I'd like him to point out buildings and landmarks along the way. He was clearly working for a good tip, but I was thankful he was friendly. It took my mind off the traffic and he really did deserve the big tip I gave him.

We finally made it to the Club Quarters Hotel in Rockefeller Center. The driver pulled up in front of the hotel to let me out. At first, I wasn't actually sure we were at the hotel. There were no signs, not even on the door. After a closer look, I saw a CQ, Club Quarters, sign on the wall next to the front doors.

Once inside, I was surprised to find a small lobby. Before I left home, my husband, Jerry, who had lived in a high-rise building in New York City for several years as a boy, reminded me that land in New York was scarce.

The clerk asked how he could help and I gave him my name and asked for a room on a lower floor. I'd always been afraid of heights and fires. He glanced up at me and back to his computer.

"How about the tenth floor?" he said.

That's what he thinks is a lower floor?

Wow! I wasn't used to being that high up. I thought the tenth floor was high, but I didn't want to ask again. I told him that would be great and thanked him.

I popped open my suitcase and hung up my clothes for the next day. Even though I had a couple of hours before I had to meet the producer and his offices were only a short walk, I wanted to arrive early to get a security clearance badge. Since I didn't know how long that would take, I left the hotel right away and found my way to 30 Rockefeller Plaza.

I actually made it to NBC studios with my security badge in plenty of time. Standing outside the studio was surreal. I'd seen it so many times on television. It caused a huge smile to form on my face. From the street, I could see the large window and desk where the anchors sat. I remembered seeing people on TV, holding up signs hoping they would get on television. Right where I was standing. The signs told where they were from and said hi to their family.

In a matter of minutes, I would get to go inside. What a thrill! How many people ever got to do that? It felt like a dream. I knew I was blessed and couldn't wait until the producer appeared and ushered me into this whole new world opening up to me.

* * *

The producer met me outside the building right on time. She unlocked several doors and took me down a narrow hallway to a small room where I met Tiffany, the other dessert contestant, and her mother, Karen. We had a lot in common, including that both of us were from Arkansas and had five children.

We made our way to the main studio, which had the large windows behind the anchors for public viewing—just like I'd seen on TV and standing outside. The kitchen was at one end of the studio. A table was set up between the studio and the kitchen for our demo. During the walk-through, I met producers, cooks, and stylists who prepared the different parts of my recipe. They explained where each ingredient would be on the table.

I was told what to do. "Explain each step and move to the next one," the producer said.

I only had two minutes to demonstrate and talk about my recipe. While the producer explained the same thing to Tiffany, I looked around the studio, checking it out. To my surprise, behind the cameras was a much smaller area than I had imagined. In front of the cameras was exactly what we see on TV.

By that point, I wasn't nervous and felt at home. Maybe it helped that I had been on our local station, KARK 4 News in Little Rock, where I was a top contestant in a barbecue sauce recipe contest.

One of the cameras was aimed in my direction. Excitement was building as I thought about being on national television. Cooking and teaching others about easy recipes are my passion. It's what I had been doing for almost a decade on my recipe blog. It's a subject I'm familiar with and comes naturally to me.

This was an opportunity to encourage others not only to bake but to do it with their children. Baking with my kids over the years created priceless memories with endless benefits.

After the walk-through, Tiffany, her mother, and I hung out. We went outside and walked around the general area, seeing Rockefeller skating rink, Tiffany's, Central Park, Trump Hotel, Radio City Music Hall, and where some of the Broadway shows were located. We got an enormous slice of New York pizza before a short walk back to the hotel.

My family has always had Friday night pizza night. Pizza makes me happy. Maybe, it's because I have special memories of making homemade pizzas with my children. Stretching the pizza dough was a fun activity even Caleb could do with his cerebral palsy.

Experiencing a famous New York pizza with my new friends was special too. I would've missed this experience if Tiffany and Karen hadn't invited me. I love talking to strangers and finding out where they are from and what they do.

My family claims I ask way too many questions, especially to strangers, and was told not to. Because my family wanted me to keep to myself, and with the fear of getting lost, I had planned to go back to the hotel. Instead, I accepted my new friends' offer to explore the city. Determined to fit in, I focused straight ahead and only talked to my new friends. We had a great time and I was thankful I didn't miss this opportunity to see New York City.

The following morning, we all walked to the TODAY Show studio for hair and makeup. We walked right past many fans gathered outside, waiting for an outdoor Mary J. Blige concert to begin. We headed straight to the guard. He checked our security pass and waved us through. He also pointed the way to hair and makeup.

While we were waiting in a small room, Mary J. Blige passed directly in front of me. She was headed to a private room. Her crew, who looked like band members, and her security team dressed in black suits stayed with us. Nobody said a word, which made it awkward. You could feel the tension in the room. I wanted to shout, "that was Mary J. Blige." In the south, I'm used to talking to everyone. I wasn't in the south and decided to keep quiet.

When it was my turn for hair and makeup, they sat me down next to actress Ellie Kemper. I could see her out of the corner of my eye when looking in the large mirror. On the other side of her were Mary J. Blige's band members and Tiffany.

I said to the lady fixing my hair, "If only these chairs could talk, I bet they would have lots of stories."

"Yes, they would," she said before becoming completely silent again.

She never asked me any questions about where I was from or why I was there. I was dying to tell her my story, but she needed to make everyone beautiful as quickly as possible. I decided to shut my big fat talkative mouth and enjoy the moment and my surroundings.

As soon as we finished, a producer was standing behind us. She was waiting to escort us to the studio. We were on in fifteen minutes, and she explained they were ready to do some pre-shots of us in the kitchen to advertise the recipe contest and demonstrations.

Sheinelle Jones anchored the segment. She entered the room right behind us and gave Tiffany and me a hug. She told us not to be nervous. She would prompt us through each step. The producer said they were ready to get a clip to promote the cooking competition. She told us to pretend like we were fighting.

During the commercial break, we were cracking up. It was so much fun.

While the clock counted down to go live, Tiffany and I said to each other, "Put your fists up."

The clock continued, three, two, one. We were live on-air. We put our fists up and pretended to be fighting.

Dylan Dryer, one of the anchors, and Ellie Kemper joined us behind the kitchen counter. They were the judges for the contest.

Tiffany was up first explaining her made-from-scratch banana upside-down cupcakes. I watched and tried to focus on what she said. By doing so, I hoped it would calm my nerves.

I felt embarrassed because my dessert was too simple. I didn't submit a made-from-scratch dessert. I started to, but I thought about the large audience the TODAY Show reached and how many people rarely cooked and had little time to bake. My submission was an easy family favorite dessert recipe.

"God," I quickly prayed, "You got me here with this simple dessert. It's not about me, but about You. Use me for Your glory."

My turn came. I started by telling everyone how quick, easy, and delicious the cake was to make. As soon as I started talking, I was no longer nervous and was having fun. I love to talk and bake. The TODAY Show gave me an outlet to do both. I tried to sell the viewers how quick and easy it was to make.

The words came easily to me. "Start with a chocolate cake mix and bake it according to the package. After the cake cools, use the back of a wooden spoon and poke holes about an inch apart all over the cake."

They had a prebaked chocolate cake in a 9x13 baking dish ready for me to poke holes. I pretended to take my frustrations out on the cake by poking holes rapidly. I asked Sheinelle if she would like to try it because it was fun, and she took me up on it.

Sheinelle said, "What do we do next?"

"Top the cake with a can of Sweetened Condensed Milk and Salted Caramel."

I reached for them and poured each one over the cake.

"They will get down in the cake to keep it moist and add flavors."

I moved over to the next cake covered with whipped topping.

"Top everything with homemade whipped topping," I explained.

I picked up the bowl of candy bars from the table.

"Finish the cake by crushing your favorite candy bars to sprinkle heavily over everything."

When I saw that the candy bars were not crushed but prechopped, I was disappointed. I wanted fine pieces to cover the whipped topping. The candy is easier to eat on the cake when crushed and not in chunks. Crushed candy covers the cake better too. I must have missed seeing the chunky pieces in the walk-through. In my local grocery stores, you can purchase a bag of Butterfingers, already crushed, in the baking aisle. I assumed they would be able to get them too or crush them themselves.

It was not that big a deal, and I was able to tell the audience to add crushed candy.

As I put the candy on the cake, Sheinelle asked me, "What is your favorite candy bar?"

I was confused. The producer told me not to mention the brand name. I hesitated because I did not know if I could answer her.

Sheinelle quickly mentioned Butterfinger, which put me at ease. I told her that's what I like on the cake.

I told her the cake made my family do a happy dance, and I hoped it made the judges do one too.

I didn't win, but it was an incredible experience. The judges loved both desserts. They said it was a difficult decision, but Tiffany's homemade ice cream with her homemade upside-down cupcake won the judges over.

A few minutes after the competition, they told us they were coming back to us for another live segment. For a few seconds, they filmed us with Sheinelle eating and enjoying both desserts. Of course, I was trying to be Miss Dramatic. After all, I was live on national television. I acted like it was the best dessert I'd ever had.

I closed my eyes and felt like I was in paradise after taking a bite. Again, it was so much fun.

Seeing Dylan Dryer and Sheinelle Jones felt unreal. Those ladies had been in my home for years through the television, and now I had the opportunity to see them in person. I was also blessed to meet Jenna Bush Hager and get my picture with her.

As we were leaving down a long narrow hall, a door was open. Jenna was in the process of having her hair colored. When our eyes met, I had to stick my head in the doorway. I said, "I am a huge fan of yours."

She replied, "I watched y'all do your demo. Y'all did a great job. You were naturals in front of the camera. Come get a picture with me."

I got a quick picture before leaving the studio. Another experience I'll never forget. Jenna is as down-to-earth and friendly as a true Texan.

Before leaving Tiffany in New York, she asked me if I had ever competed at the World Food Championships. The WFC. When I said no and asked what it was, she told me.

"The World Food Championships is a five-day cooking competition where the best chefs and home cooks from all over the world compete in three rounds of cooking. Each Category Champion wins $7,500. Category champions compete again at the Final Table, where they could win the World Food Champion title and an additional $100,000. WFC includes ten categories with forty-five head cooks in each category. The categories include Bacon, Barbecue, Burger, Dessert, Rice/Noodle, Sandwich, Seafood, Soup, Steak, and Vegetarian."

Tiffany encouraged me to check it out. I promised I would, then hugged my new friend goodbye.

* * *

The whole trip was a whirlwind, and I was back to the airport before I knew it.

A lady approached me and said, "Excuse me, were you on the TO-DAY Show this morning?"

I grinned and said yes.

"I saw you demonstrating a recipe," she said. "You did a great job!"

"Thank you!" I replied.

She continued, "Was this your first time?"

"Yes, and it was a lot of fun. My dessert recipe was in the top two in a contest. I won an opportunity to demonstrate it live."

"You were a natural."

Her words were so encouraging. I felt comfortable because I had been meeting with ladies from my church. We met weekly in my home, and I encouraged them with quick and easy recipe demonstrations. I love talking about food and helping others.

My plane left New York on time, and we landed in Little Rock. Casey, my oldest son, picked me up, and we made it to Carly's ceremony with no time to spare. Thankfully, it hadn't begun, and Jerry, Floy, Caleb, and Diana saved me a seat.

I was so proud of Carly for working relentless hours through medical school. I was constantly thanking God for working everything out for me to have the experience of a lifetime and get to see my daughter on her special day.

I felt God's overwhelming love as he worked everything out for me.

CHAPTER TWO

WORLD FOOD
CHAMPIONSHIPS

Every accomplishment starts with the decision to try.

"I don't qualify," I told my husband, Jerry.

After looking up the requirements to compete at the World Food Championships, I discovered you must win a competition and receive a golden ticket. Neither of which had happened for me.

World Food Championships only hand out golden tickets at select competitions. Jerry got on the computer and clicked more links.

"It looks like they have ten categories," he said. "They have forty contestants in each category and a wildcard in each. That's your shot. You were born to compete."

"I'll check it out," I said, still skeptical.

When I spoke to the WFC, the man who answered the phone said, "The only wildcard slot left is in desserts. Fill out the information online and pay the entrance fee, and you're in."

I was thrilled to have a chance to compete against the best chefs and home cooks in the world. A part of me always wanted to be a chef, especially a pastry chef, and WFC gave me the chance to be one. The other part of me was scared to compete against professionals. I knew I had a lot I didn't know.

The contest was the second week of November 2017 in Orange Beach, Alabama. I grew up nearby in Mobile, so it felt like I was going home. That's where I learned and practiced baking. I especially enjoyed baking easy desserts for my dad and siblings.

My dad would say things like, "Dinner is delicious! Did you bake us something special tonight?" Like he really looked forward to it. That encouraged me to continue cooking and baking.

When I questioned if entering the WFC was worth the registration fee, my husband, Jerry said, "What could it hurt? It'll be a great experience to cook against professionals, chefs, and other home cooks. You love baking, are extremely organized, and are the most competitive person I know. I have no doubt you can do this."

That was Jerry. Always encouraging and believing in me. I filled out the form, paid my fee, and was all set to compete at the World Food Championships.

* * *

November 2017

When I entered the World Food Championships tent for the first time with the other dessert competitors, I wondered what I was doing there. The other contestants had to win a sanctioned contest to compete at this level. I'd never won anything nor competed in a WFC sanctioned event.

The sea of chef coats was intimidating. I'd seen a list of the names and bios of my competitors. They were trained chefs and pastry chefs who worked full-time in restaurants and bakeries. The home cooks were bloggers or had side jobs baking and selling their treats. They were all way better trained than I was.

The competition consisted of two rounds of baking back-to-back. The first round was the Structured Build. In that round, all competitors made the same type of dish. That year it was a Swiss Roll. I'd chosen my flavorful Caramel Apple Swiss Roll. A family favorite.

We had one hour to make it. At the one-hour mark, the turn-in clock started. We had ten minutes to get our dessert on the turn-in table.

The second round was the Signature Round. The competitors could choose their own dessert to make. Pumpkin Praline Layer cake was my choice. It bursts with warm spices. We had forty minutes from the end of the first turn-in to begin the second dessert and ten minutes to have it on the table.

If I turned the dish in late, I'd be disqualified. That seemed crazy to me. I was an amateur home cook. I'd never worked under extreme pressure to complete a recipe.

Earlier in the day, I watched the bacon and seafood categories compete. That gave me some insight on what to expect. Clearly, the clock was the main competitor, and it never stopped. I had to be prepared to think quickly on my feet for alternative plans if something went wrong.

The doubts engulfed me, but the chefs inspired me.

My passion for cooking had to overcome their formal training. My family always said I was super competitive. Maybe they're right. I was going to do my best and let God do the rest. I quoted this to my kids often. It was my time to live it out.

The head chefs gathered around for a cooks' meeting before the competition began. The meeting was to remind us of the rules and for the organizers to answer any questions. Everyone listened intently to every word, especially me, since this was my first time competing.

The other Chefs had their game faces on, and it was obvious they were there to win.

The tension in the room could be cut with a knife. No pun intended. Eyebrows were furrowed as if they were deep in thought. They had straight faces. Not a cheerful countenance among them.

I could feel the tension rising within me. The room was hot, and my face was turning red. I took a few deep breaths and slowly blew them out while listening to the *cheferees*, referees in food sport, give us the instructions.

After the cooks' meeting, they gave me the number twenty-three, representing my kitchen station. My heart dropped when I saw my unlucky number twenty-three. Not the number I would've chosen.

We had fifteen minutes to set up our work areas. Film crews and media roamed all over the place. Contestants raced to find their kitchens, set them up, then meet with their sous-chefs, who had arms full of kitchen supplies.

My two sous-chefs were my husband, Jerry, and my sister-in-law, Marsha. I held up my number for them to see and gave them a frown. Didn't matter. Nothing I could do about it, so I prepared to go to work.

I raced to my station along with everyone else. Jerry and Marsha were right behind me. Their hands were full. Marsha dragged a cooler full of butter, eggs, heavy cream, and plenty of ice.

Jerry pulled a jumbo-sized toolbox full of cooking ingredients, baking pans, and gadgets we needed for the two recipes we were about to prepare. Our kitchen space included a nine-by-nine area with one table. It had a microwave and mixer on it and another table was used for workspace. I found Gotham Steel pots and pans, an electric range, plus a Bull Grill in the kitchen in my supplies.

My cooking gadgets and ingredients were all labeled. This made setup relatively easy. We weren't allowed to open any ingredients nor have premade ingredients on hand. We were told to bring receipts in case a cheferee wanted us to prove we purchased an ingredient.

During the setup, *cheferees* roamed around looking for open packages and premade ingredients. While getting the supplies in order, one approached me. He wanted to see my receipt. Thank God I was prepared to quickly show him, not only the receipt, but the exact ingredient he was looking for.

I'd taken the time to color code and make notes on my receipts. My attention to details paid off that day. The cheferee was satisfied and left as fast as he showed up. After he left, we huddled for a quick prayer before our set-up time was over.

After that, we had about a minute before we began cooking. I took the opportunity to look around the room and take in all the excitement. Fear overwhelmed me again as I saw chefs from all over the world.

Marsha saw the fear in my eyes and said, "We're against the clock and not them. We got this. Stick to the plans."

The words were encouraging and calmed my nerves some. Marsha is a fabulous cook. I wanted her to be one of my sous-chefs for that very reason. Because of her positive attitude and determination.

Marsha is a three-time cancer survivor. She got breast cancer when she was thirty-four and was raising two small children. Cancer had come back two times in other parts of her body. Marsha not only survived everything but has the most upbeat and encouraging attitude. I knew she'd be such an asset to my team.

The announcer started counting down. "10, 9, 8, . . . 3, 2, 1 . . . start!"

A resolve rose up inside of me. Cooking was my passion, and I was there to prove I could cook. Once the countdown started, I stopped looking around and focused on my dessert. I had memorized everything I planned on accomplishing and was ready to start the first steps.

My oldest daughter, Carly, was the one who encouraged me to make my Caramel Apple Swiss Roll, one of her favorites. She'd always been my toughest critic when judging my food. I respected her opinion and knew it helped me to be a better cook. When she loved one of my recipes, I was reassured that I had something special.

The next few minutes were a blur, but I felt calm and focused. I quickly started with the wet ingredients. I separated six large eggs. The egg whites went in a stand mixer for Jerry to whip. I used the yolks.

Separating the eggs took great care. If I got even a speck of yolk in my whites, they would not whip correctly. With a hand mixer and a large bowl, I whipped the egg yolks until tripled in size. I gradually added a half cup of sugar to the yolks and continued beating until pale and thick.

Jerry whipped the egg white mixture and ensured the oven was set to 375 degrees. On medium-high speed, he whipped the egg whites with a half teaspoon of cream of tartar until soft peaks formed. To determine soft peaks, he turned the whisk over. At home, I had shown him to watch for a peak shape. It's loose and melts back into the mix after a few seconds.

Next, Jerry slowly added a half cup of sugar to the egg whites and continued beating until stiff peaks. Stiff peaks form when you lift your beater, and you get a nice peak that holds its shape. At that point, Jerry stopped the mixer. He thought they were stiff and called me over for a look.

"Perfect," I said.

Marsha measured and sifted the dry ingredients. Sifting the flour was an extra step but allowed for an accurate measurement. It also made for a lighter textured cake. Sifting all the dry ingredients helped the cake not to have any clumps.

Here's the recipe:

1-1/4 cup sifted cake flour

1-1/4 teaspoons baking powder

1 teaspoon salt

1 tablespoons Apple Pie Spice

The taste was fifty percent of the scoring, so spices were critical. I wanted to get a lot of spices in the cake without taking the time to open many time-consuming containers. Small containers can be tedious. That's why I decided to go with apple pie spice.

After the wet and dry ingredients, I gently stirred a third of the whites into the batter. Stirring the whites loosens up the egg yolk mixture. I could then gently fold the remaining whites without deflating them. A sponge cake needed to be light and fluffy. Stirring a small portion of stiff whites before folding the rest helped keep them that way.

I checked the time.

So far so good.

I quickly put the batter into a 13- x 17-inch baking sheet lined with parchment paper getting it as level as possible. In the oven it went for fifteen minutes. I set two timers. My watch timer and the oven timer to make sure it cooked the right amount of time.

The noise level in the kitchen arena was as loud as a football stadium. With the combination of everyone's kitchen timers, mixers, blenders, talking, plus the loud music, you could not hear. I was afraid I wouldn't even hear the oven timer.

Since the Swiss roll only needed fifteen minutes in the oven, we all hurried to make the caramel apple mousse filling, get the toppings prepared, and make the apple roses for plating.

The apple roses were time-consuming. We cored seven large Gala apples and sliced them thin using a mandolin. Thin slices allowed the apples to cook faster and be easily rolled. If too much heat was added, they'd lose the beautiful red color. The color stood out on the roses like the tips of a real flower.

Apple roses were a tedious procedure, but they're beautiful and worth the effort. I began by rolling one slice tight. Another piece was wrapped loosely around the centerpiece. This process continued by overlapping the previous slice until I had the size of the rose I desired.

We made one for each judge's plate, plus four large apple roses for the display plate.

After a few minutes, something told me to check on the cake in the oven. Thank God I did! The oven had shut off. Jerry climbed under the table to see if everything was plugged in while I called for help. The *cheferee* was quickly at our kitchen and got the power back on in just a few minutes.

The cake had less than five minutes left to bake, so I watched it constantly. It appeared to be rising. I was careful not to open the oven door in the chaos. Baking time was everything when getting a sponge cake to roll without cracking. It's impossible to rollup if it's the least bit under or overbaked.

In fact, as many times as I had made this cake at home, it only rolled up once without any cracks.

When to open the oven door was basically a total guess.

I stared through the oven window and told myself, *I can do all things through Christ who gives me strength.*

I opened the door.

This was the moment of truth.

I touched the cake and it sprung back.

It was ready!

I quickly took it out of the oven. Relieved, I shouted, "It looks good!"

My sous-chefs cheered. I ran a knife around the edges and flipped it over on a towel dusted with confectioners' sugar. At that time, someone put a microphone in front of me and asked me what I was making. I looked up, put on a big smile, and quickly answered his questions.

Excitement continued to build in me as the dessert was coming together.

The next step was to remove the parchment paper and slowly roll the cake up. This was the tricky part.

It cracked!

Lots of media people roamed around the arena. Someone from the media, *Big Time Entertainment*, had his camera on my cake. My heart sank, certain he'd gotten the whole disaster on film.

Thankfully, the crack was small and on one end, so I hoped to save it.

After finishing rolling up the cake, I placed it in the cooler for a quick cool down. The well of the cooler had bags of ice on the bottom and sides. I also lined foil on the inside of the well, hoping this would keep the cake from touching moisture, and help it to cool faster.

We began getting the turn-in plates ready for the five judges along with the display plate. Once it had twenty minutes to cool, I unrolled the cake, and we began to add the layer of filling and roll the cake back up.

The next step was to pour the caramel on the outside of the cake, cover the caramel with salted chopped pecans, and decorate it with apple roses. It was a lot to get done with only fifteen minutes left in the first round of the competition. Especially when that included the ten-minute turn-in window, which began in five minutes!

The announcer came on the loudspeaker. It was time to start turning in our desserts. We were to make our way to the front of the tent and place our dessert on the table. The small crack was at one end of the dessert. So, I started cutting my five judges' samples from that end and plated them.

The judges' samples were for taste and execution-only. The display plate was what judges used for the appearance points.

I took the remaining seven inches of the Caramel Apple Swiss Roll, carefully lifted it with a large spatula, and placed it upright on a display plate with apple roses on it. I quickly rushed the large platter with the five samples and the display plate to the tent and placed it on the table.

Once the dessert hit the turn-in table, I couldn't touch it. The judges were in a tent behind the turn-in table. It's there that they sampled our dishes.

The judges used the E.A.T. methodology: Execution, Appearance, and Taste. This allowed competition categories, including Bacon, Barbecue, Burger, Dessert, Rice/Noodle, Sandwich, Seafood, Soup, Steak, and Vegetarian to be judged with the same consistent criteria.

Execution made up thirty-five percent of the score, appearance, fifteen percent, and taste fifty percent.

A cheferee picked up the tray and carried it to the judges' tent. I raced back to my kitchen and began working on my next dessert—the Signature Dish round where I was to make a Praline Pumpkin Cake.

The countdown clock was ticking. Faster than I would've liked.

Marsha started the dry ingredients for the cake. I started the wet ingredients and then combined the dry and wet ingredients while she prepared the pans.

Jerry preheated the oven, opened most of our ingredients, and started whipping the butter for the buttercream.

After putting the cake in the oven, we all took turns checking on it. The praline pumpkin cake round went much smoother. I was able to turn everything in as soon as the turn-in window opened.

The three-layer cake with caramel buttercream and praline pecans looked beautiful. The flavor was outstanding. I knew no matter how the cake scored that I had done my best. I was so proud of my team, who had worked hard. I could have never accomplished this dream without the best sous-chefs. They tackled everything I asked them to do and more. We were all exhausted but took time for hugs and pictures to celebrate our accomplishment before cleaning up the messy kitchen.

At that point, everything was in the hands of the judges.

CHAPTER THREE

THE TOP TEN COUNTDOWN

The next chapter of your life is going to be amazing.

Dessert was the last competition of the day. The top ten in each category were to be announced. We packed up our supplies and dirty dishes, cleaned up our kitchen, and headed to the large outdoor stage.

We were all exhausted. We sat down on a curb and waited for the results. Mike McCloud, the President, and C.E.O. of the World Food Championships, called the top ten from each of the categories.

Caleb sat next to me. I thanked him for helping me practice at home. If we made it into the top ten, it was because he helped. Leading up to the competition, Caleb and I baked more Swiss rolls than we could ever eat.

A few weeks before the World Food Championships, my oven went out. I was devastated at first. I knew it would take a while to replace, and I wouldn't be able to practice my Swiss roll again. The new oven was installed the day before leaving for WFC, so we didn't get to practice again.

I'd already packed up my supplies for the competition, but I was thankful for all the preparation we did to prepare. Had I waited until the last few weeks to practice, I would've been scrambling and wouldn't have felt as prepared as I did leading into the competition.

Another way God was watching out for me. A reminder that I had to stop relying totally on my abilities and keep trusting God.

Caleb helped me take our Swiss rolls to neighbors, the fire station, and we even sent some to prisoners. He loved going with me to deliver our desserts. When we gave a dessert to a neighbor or friend, we reconnected. Found out about what they had been doing. We told them about the competition and asked them to pray for us.

They said they would. Caleb gave them an instantaneous smile. He loves to bake and knows where everything is in the kitchen. When we are baking, I say to Caleb, "Every chef has a sous-chef, and you are my number one sous-chef."

I let him know he had an important job, practicing with me so I could compete at WFC. Each time, his confidence exploded as he stood tall as Superman with his hands on his hips.

I gave him a hug. Everything was so fast paced at the World Food Championships, that I didn't have as much time for him. At home, I could take the time to give him all the hugs he wanted. He's such a loving child and will stand in your way until he can give you a hug.

God uses him to teach our family to slow down and show love. Due to the time limit, his short-term memory loss and seizures, he can't compete as my sous-chef at WFC. That didn't mean he wasn't a valuable part of our team.

Shortly after nine that night, Mike began announcing the top ten finalists in the dessert category. The top ten would compete the next day for first place in the dessert. The World Food Champion in dessert would compete at the final table with the other first-place winners of each specialty for the World Food Champion title and $100,000.

I knew my desserts tasted like heaven in my mouth but still doubted it could ever beat a chef. I figured if I had a chance to get into the top ten in dessert, it would be around tenth place. Even so, a tenth-place finish would get me a golden ticket to compete the following year. It would also give me the assurance I could bake.

Mike called out the top ten in desserts.

Tenth place. He didn't call my name.

Number nine and eight were called and they weren't me. Then number seven.

My heart sank. I figured seven was as high as I could get. The disappointment hit me like a semi-truck on a freeway. I placed my face on my knees and slumped down on the curb. I just wanted the top ten announcements to be over.

We prepared to go back to the room. The whole team was disappointed. My mother-in-law, Floy, was cold. Caleb was tired and leaned on my shoulder. Jerry, and Marsha, who worked so hard, were all exhausted.

All that effort had been for nothing.

The next numbers were called. Six. Five. Four. Three.

They couldn't get this over fast enough.

Mike called the top ten to the stage. I felt a twinge of bitterness. I knew number twenty-three would be unlucky. I should have quit as soon as they handed me that cursed number.

I was born on the twenty-third, and as a child, my birthday was not celebrated. My mother was an alcoholic and left our family when I was fourteen years old. I don't remember her ever saying "I love you" or "Happy Birthday" or ever hugging me. That's why I hated the number.

Once I got married, my husband's company had their annual kick-off meeting held every year during the week of my birthday, which caused him to miss my birthday for decades. Then there was a horrible ice storm that knocked out power one year on my birthday and another birthday that led to me getting twenty-two stitches, which, I guess, was better than twenty-three.

Most years, I tried my hardest to just get through every January 23rd.

Mike continued the count down. He said, "Before I announce who's in first place, I want to say that this person scored a rare perfect score in the Swiss Roll competition."

I was thinking, *How could anyone do that?*

"And the winner is,"

I heard my name.

What?

"Diane Roark!"

Could there be two people with my name?

My brain couldn't understand what I was hearing. The crowd erupted. There was so much noise from people yelling and clapping that I couldn't hear. On top of that, they cranked up the music.

Surely I was hearing things.

Then I saw my name on the huge jumbo screen. It flashed the entire length of the stage.

Jerry shouted, "You did it!"

Finally, it registered. I won!

A perfect score?

I jumped up and down like a schoolgirl.

Wrapped my arms around Jerry and gave him a massive hug for putting up with me being an excessively, compulsive organizer, and sometimes demanding when practicing and preparing for WFC.

Next, I grabbed Caleb and Marsha and thanked them for their help. I told Jerry, Caleb, and Marsha I couldn't have done it without them. Then reminded them we couldn't have done it without God.

"Please thank God for this win," I said to them.

Caleb was ecstatic. He whispered, "God, did the rest."

At that moment, I felt God's love like never before. Caleb reminded me of what I always told him. When he struggled to do so many things due to his cerebral palsy, I told him to do his best and let God do the rest.

After walking up on stage, I told Mr. McCloud how thankful I was for the opportunity to compete. I let him know I was a home cook with no competitive cooking experience.

He hugged me and said, "You did it. I'm proud of you."

He put the top ten medal around my neck. I felt even more love as each of the competitors congratulated me.

The moment was surreal, and I didn't want it to end.

We were all suddenly not so tired, as adrenaline shot through us like we'd gotten B-12 shots.

On the way to the car, I heard my name and turned around. Following behind me was a chef who competed in the dessert category. She asked me about my secrets to the perfect score recipe.

Someone was asking me for advice!

I mentioned almost apologetically that I was a home cook, and this was my first time competing at WFC. My recipe was one I'd prepared many times, but I kicked the flavor and the plating way up. I also made sure to mention my team.

She congratulated me again and we got in the car and left.

"Marsha," I said, "I feel God's love like never before."

She nodded.

"That woman who stopped me wanted to know how I got a perfect score. I'm in no way as talented or qualified as she is. God must be with us."

Then it hit me.

Being in the top ten in dessert meant that I had to cook the next day. I had no idea what I was going to make. Honestly, I never in my wildest dreams thought I'd win and be cooking on the second day.

The infused ingredient was apples. That much I did know.

When we got back to the R.V., my mother-in-law helped Jerry do the dishes while I worked on a recipe for the next day's competition. It had to be entered into the computer by midnight.

I ran several ideas by Marsha, but nothing clicked until we talked about my apple cake topped with my Southern Fried Apples in the shape of a giant rose. I baked that cake with my kids every fall for years.

That made sense. The taste of the apple cake was a winner, and adding the apple rose to cover the top would be stunning. Marsha loved the idea too.

The next day, we practiced baking the apple cake in the R.V. The oven was tiny, and the cake barely fit in it. Full of apples and spices, it made the RV smell amazing. When the cake finished baking, I planned to set it on the top of the three-burner gas stove to allow it to cool. As soon as I took the cake out, I began feeling the heat through the potholders.

I tried to put the cake down quickly, but the burners were higher than I thought. I missed them. The next thing I knew, the cake was upside down on the R.V. floor. I removed the cake pan from the cake. Removing the pan from a hot upside-down cake caused it to collapse all over the floor.

There was no saving the cake.

My heart sank.

The doubts flooded my emotions like a river floods a canyon after a torrential rain. I shouldn't be there trying to cook with professionals.

With the cake on the floor, I had no idea how it was going to taste. I found a piece that hadn't hit the floor and tore off a small bit. It wasn't bad. I had added more spices than usual which made the flavor even better.

Instead of remaking the cake, we continued to make the fried apples. To practice the apple rose, I designed it on a plate. It looked beautiful, and I was excited about the taste, and look of the cake.

Feeling better now that I had practiced it.

It was a hot day for a dessert competition. So, I carried my butter in a separate bag and not in the cooler. The butter needed to be at room temperature to mix the batter.

The other categories competed throughout the day. I bided my time by watching them. It helped to calm my nerves. It was difficult to tell how soft the butter was getting through the unopened container of four sticks.

Unfortunately, the butter had gotten too soft. The batter wasn't the texture it would typically be. A WFC sponsor, the Challenge Butter, had additional butter in the pantry and I could've gotten some from them. But I would have wasted time getting the butter, plus the refrigerated butter would have been too cold.

I wasn't upset. I'd already won and exceeded my expectations. Whatever happened from then on out was gravy. God had allowed me to do more than I could've ever imagined in the first year at WFC. How could I be disappointed?

I ended up finishing in third place. In my first year competing. I wouldn't be moving on to the final table, but I did receive a golden ticket to compete in 2018.

The experience was a thrill of a lifetime.

I've always been a dreamer, and after my first WFC competition, I set a big dream and goals to someday win the dessert category at the World Food Championships.

God had worked things out for me beyond what I could have ever done, by giving me ideas and calming my fears. The whole experience was somewhat of a spiritual awakening for me. For the first time in a long time, I knew God had a plan for my life to use me for His glory.

"If God is for us, who is against us?" (Romans 8:31 ASV)

God was for me. It felt like I had experienced that verse for the first time in my life. God wanted me to succeed, and He was pulling for me.

"Now to him who is able to do exceedingly abundantly above all that we ask or think, according to the power that works in us." (Ephesians 3:20 WEB)

Little did I know that this was just the beginning.

CHAPTER FOUR

SECOND & THIRD YEAR
AT WFC

Sometimes you win, sometimes you learn.

Between my first and second year of competing, I took a World Food Championships E.A.T certified class to become a judge. The instructor said the A in E.A.T. was for appearance and should be judged first.

An "appearance dish" was passed in front of us to judge.

"Give the dish a score from one to ten, one being inedible and ten outstanding," the instructor said. "Is it pleasing to the eye? Do you want to take a big bite out of it right now?"

The first thing I noticed was the chef took great care to place the steak directly in the center of the plate on a bed of lobster mashed potatoes. I could see chunks of the lobster. The herb wine reduction sauce trickled on the mashed potatoes. Tiny pieces of the herbs were in the sauce. On top of the sauce was a sprig of thyme. On the outer edge of one side of the plate were bright orange dots. I assumed they were likely from the carrot reduction.

The other side of the plate had brightly colored green beans with slivers of carrots. It looked stunning, and I wanted a bite. I examined the plate closely as it passed by to find any flaws, including burnt places on the steak or smudges on the plate.

I wrote down my appearance score.

Next was the execution score. On the scorecard was the title and the short description filled out by the chef. I needed to make sure everything the chef said he was going to do was completed or executed properly. If he said the steak was cooked medium, it needed to be medium. Did the sauce break? Did the chef mash the potatoes? Did all the food get on the plate? Did he add the dots of carrot reduction around the plate? Were the green beans cooked al dente, or were they soggy?

I examined the dish closely and wrote down my score.

Finally, I was ready to move on to the taste which made up fifty percent of the total score. The instructor gave us some helpful instructions

"Don't base taste on your likes and dislikes. Are the flavors balanced? Do they work together to create a unique depth of flavors? Do you want another bite?"

The chef said he used lobster, rosemary, thyme, and a wine reduction. I noticed all of those smells, and even lobster. I took a bite and chewed it slowly searching for each of the flavors and how well they went together.

After taking another bite, I was ready to give the dish a "Taste" score. Scoring cards were collected and tabulated.

The score given that day is not the reason I'm sharing this. This judging experience was eye-opening. It helped me understand what the judges were looking for in my dishes. I left there exhilarated and couldn't wait to compete at the World Food Championships in November.

* * *

2018 World Food Championships

As I prepared my dessert for my second trip to the WFC, I heard my family members yelling my name from the audience. Carly, Caleb, Floy, my sister Daisy, my niece Jenny and her family, my niece Elizabeth and her family, cousins including Annie's family, Jerry's cousins Steve and Dennis and his family, were all cheering for me.

Having that many people cheering me on was a new experience for me. I played five years of volleyball during high school and middle school and swam on the swim team and no family member ever attended a single event. Not even my mom and dad. If it weren't for my husband, who was my boyfriend at the time, I never would've had anyone cheering me on.

It warmed my heart to see everyone there. It was a humbling feeling to know my family took the time to drive to see me compete. I teared up and felt like I'd already won.

The second year competing at WFC was just as special as my first year. Annie, my cousin, a talented cake decorator, and Marsha, who encouraged me from the beginning, were my sous-chefs this time. I was pleased with our team and more optimistic that I would be successful than I had been the first year.

The competitor in me quickly got my head in the game, and I got busy preparing my recipes. It helped that I had the previous experience from the first competition to draw on.

For the first round, the Structured Round, everyone prepared a tart. Since I'd done well with my apple recipes the first year, I decided on a caramel apple tart. Annie and Marsha started by making the crust and preparing the filling while I cut, sliced, and cooked twelve apples.

One of the most exciting times in the competition is the countdown. At least it is if you are finished with your dish. We were, and the tarts were gorgeous. My heart warmed when I heard everyone counting down and my family cheering.

I raced to the turn-in table with just under a minute to spare.

I hurried back to my assigned kitchen. Marsha and Annie were working on the batter for the Apple Praline Cake. I began cutting and preparing more apples. Twenty minutes later, I checked on the cake.

Something was wrong.

I grabbed the temperature gun to check the oven. It wasn't up to the correct temperature.

After showing the cheferees, they asked if I would like to move the cake to a preheated spare oven. Now, I had a huge quick decision to make. I decided to let the cake continue baking. If the cake were still warm when transporting it to the judges, it would be okay, as I didn't plan on adding buttercream to the center layers of the cake. When I flipped the cake over, the indulgent praline pecan layer would be in the middle. The gooey praline layer would act like glue and buttercream would melt between the layers causing the cake to tumble.

With ten minutes to spare, I removed it from the oven ten minutes later than I had planned. It smelled terrific. The judges' tasting portion, the single-layer cakes, looked beautiful, and so did the two-layer appearance cake.

Satisfied, I walked the cake to the judges' tent. On the way, things changed. Because the cake was still warm, even hot, the top layer slid off. Now, I had another quick decision to make. Did I juggle the tray of cakes with one hand and try to slide the cake back over or did I place the tray on the table and trust God?

Remember, once it was on the table, I couldn't touch it or I'd be disqualified. The doubts I felt in the first competition began to flood my mind.

Why did I bake another cake?

What was I thinking?

I couldn't risk ruining the cake altogether by trying to fix it on the fly. I put the tray down, determined to learn from my poor decisions. Back at the kitchen I told my sous-chefs what had happened.

We were all disappointed but hoped for the best. As I told them, it was all in God's hands. The flavor of the apple praline cake would be hard to beat.

God overwhelmed me again when Mike McCloud called my name for another rare perfect score on my Apple Tart. I also won bonus bucks—extra money—by using an ingredient from the sponsor, *The Jelly Queens*.

The room was standing room only and noisy, but I could hear my family cheer for me when Mike called out my perfect score. It was an incredible feeling and having my family there to share my experience made it like icing on the cake. Pun intended.

Winning was special, but to me, giving someone your time is the best way to show love. It's always a sweet feeling to win but having a win and family telling you they are proud of you is a feeling I never knew I was missing.

With my perfect score in the first round and my apple praline cake's high score on taste, I made it to the top ten. I moved on to the next round in fifth place.

Do you remember Tiffany, the other contestant on the TODAY show? The one who beat me in the live competition. While standing on the stage, I heard Mike call Tiffany's name. I was thrilled for my friend who had encouraged me to enter WFC in the first place. It felt good to be standing on the stage together.

In the top ten dessert round, I made several mistakes. My decision to bake another cake in the short one-hour time limit was problematic. With little time left, I removed the cake from the oven and took it out of the pans to cool down with only fifteen minutes remaining.

I had no choice but to frost the cake. The cake was warm, and I knew the buttercream would melt and the top layer would slide off.

I used the infused sponsored ingredient, Walmart's Rosé, to make a Strawberry Rosé cake with a Strawberry Rosé Buttercream. It was the best cake and buttercream I'd ever had, taste wise. Both the strawberry and rosé flavors exploded in your mouth, which was great since taste was fifty percent of the score. But the cake was the worst decorating job I'd ever done.

Just like the second round, as I made the walk to the turn-in table, the larger cake began to slide. The buttercream in the middle of the cake melted, and the top layer was only sitting on half of the bottom layer. I made the same decision and sat it down on the table anyway.

The lessons learned that year were invaluable. I was not so much disappointed in my mistakes as determined to learn from them and improve my baking and competitive baking skills. The biggest lesson was that the only competition is the clock. The clock never stops. I had to get better at anticipating what could go wrong and have a backup plan for everything.

I finished in fifth place overall. I was disappointed at first, but not for long because I remembered my golden ticket. Despite my failures, God had worked things out. I had many things to be thankful for. I thanked Him for my family being here, for the top-five finish, and receiving another golden ticket. With that ticket, I could relax knowing I didn't have to win a competition to compete the following year at the World Food Championships.

After two appearances on the world's biggest cooking stage, I had two top-five finishes and two perfect scores in the dessert category.

I felt God's overwhelming love for me once again. I couldn't have done it without His strength.

"Oh give thanks to the God of heaven; for his loving kindness endures forever." (Psalm 136:26 WEB)

* * *

2019 World Food Championships

The next year, the World Food Championships moved from Orange Beach, Alabama, to Dallas, Texas.

In the first round—the Signature Round—everyone had to make stuffed cookies for the challenge.

I was excited.

Caleb and I had been baking cookies since before he could walk. I would sit him on the kitchen counter and make cookies or pound cakes every week. Baking with Caleb was a fun way to help him with his memory. We practiced the same recipes at least once a week for decades. He eventually memorized the chocolate chip cookie and pound cake recipes.

After hearing stuffed cookies was the challenge at WFC, Caleb and I baked cookies several times a week. We started with our favorite chocolate chip cookie recipe and stuffed it. With each batch of cookies, we changed the filling to see which one tasted the best, had the gooiest center, and looked the prettiest.

We tested several different kinds of caramels and chocolates in our cookies to achieve the gooiest texture. Each cookie was delicious, but I didn't think they were World Food Championship worthy mainly because the centers weren't extremely gooey. Therefore, we got busy testing different sugar cookies with various gooey centers.

Since none of them were special enough for the World Food Championships, we moved on to practicing combinations using Snickerdoodles. As soon as I took a bite of my Snickerdoodle cookies stuffed with caramel and apple pie filling, I knew I had a winner. Family, neighbors, and friends all confirmed after one bite that we had a hit. It tasted like biting into a caramel apple, but better. The inside was gooey caramel and spiced apple filling. I got a crunch from the cookie and the salted pecans.

Caramel Apple Snickerdoodles stuffed with caramel and home-made apple pie filling were going to be my Structured Round. Those cookies were also beautifully decorated with apple roses.

My Caramel Apple Tart was going to be my second-round dessert. The Signature Round. Both desserts had the potential to win. I just prayed I wouldn't make any mistakes. When baking at such a fast pace, anything could go wrong like it had several times in the past.

We were in the hotel packing the cooler to head downstairs for the competition. I took the butter out of the refrigerator and put it into a bag to carry separately as it needed to be at room temperature. The butter was hard when we left the hotel. When we got to the competition, I decided to place the butter on the bleachers to thaw, since they were in the sun.

As the dessert competitors were arriving, I looked around at all the new faces. I remembered how nervous I was in 2017, my first year competing. Now, I felt my role was to greet and help answer any questions for the first-time competitors.

I was able to warn them about how loud it is in the kitchen arena.

"It's extremely difficult to communicate with your sous chefs, hear your oven timer, or even the countdown clock."

"Make sure you understand what each other is saying."

"Make sure you pay close attention to your oven not only to hear the timer but to see if it is on. I have lost power in the past."

"If you lose power, the cheferees are quick to help you."

When I finished greeting everyone, it was time for the cooks' meeting. I picked up my butter and headed to the meeting. I already knew what to expect and was anxious to get started.

We got set up and it was time to bake. I'm always a little nervous at first, but once we start baking, I'm in my comfort zone. There's nothing quite like it. Every year, I have so much fun baking at the World Food Championships. I get a rush of adrenaline and a lot of energy while racing against a clock.

I started by creaming together one cup of butter and 1-1/2 cups of sugar. The sugar and butter didn't cream together light and fluffy. I could have run to the WFC pantry and grabbed butter provided by Challenge Butter, but I figured I would lose too much time, plus the butter would be too cold. It was in a refrigerator but needed to be at room temperature. I decided not to get new butter and used the butter I had.

After creaming the butter and sugar, I added the two eggs one at a time, mixing well after each one. I added two tablespoons of milk and two teaspoons of pure vanilla and mixed until blended.

Jerry preheated the oven to 325 degrees, got started on the caramel, and sliced the apples on the mandolin to make apple roses. While I creamed the butter and sugar, Marsha started whisking the dry ingredients.

3 cups all-purpose flour

2 teaspoons cream of tartar

1-1/2 teaspoon baking soda

3/4 teaspoon salt

After combining the wet and dry ingredients. I combined the remaining half cup of sugar plus two teaspoons of ground cinnamon and two teaspoons of ground apple pie spice. Marsha and I scooped out the dough using an ice cream scoop. We stuffed a small scoop of apple pie filling and caramel into each cookie and rolled the cookies thoroughly in the sugar and spice mixture. We placed the balls two inches apart on a baking sheet lined with parchment paper and baked for about fifteen minutes or until slightly tan around the edges.

The cookies spread more than normal during the baking process. I could have overcome this problem by putting the cookies in the freezer for a few minutes, but time didn't allow it. After cooling, I topped the cookies with additional caramel, and an apple rose. I picked out the prettiest one and the best shaped cookie possible to be judged for appearance.

I knew the taste was spot on, and we did our best. It was time to let God do the rest.

The second-round tart with the big apple rose design was gorgeous but leaned slightly on one side. To have additional time to cut and arrange the apple slices for the roses, I decided not to bake my spiced cookie crust. I would've had to wait for the crust to cool before filling and designing the rose. Instead, I tossed the crust in the cooler for a few minutes to harden it up.

When I went to take the tart out of the ten-inch pan, a small portion fell on one side from the weight of the caramel, mousse, and the beautiful apple rose. My heart sank. This tart would be judged on appearance. I knew this was not World Food Championship standards, and I would get points taken off.

Cutting corners and not baking the crust was going to cost me.

When am I going to learn from my mistakes?

I had prepared this tart many times, and I was positive the flavor was a winner. The apple tart had a perfect score the previous year, so I hoped to make it into the top ten despite the appearance problems.

My family and I sat on the lawn in front of Reunion Tower in downtown Dallas and listened to Mike count down the dessert contestants. I was losing hope. He had not called my name. It looked like I hadn't even made the top ten.

Over the years, I had become good friends with several contestants, so I cheered for them and genuinely excited to see each of my friends moving on, but I thought, *It's not my year.*

The devil was constantly in my head. He was telling me how I was not as good as everyone else. That I didn't belong.

Blah. Blah. Blah. All the same stuff he told me the year before. He liked to throw those doubts in my head when I was most vulnerable to them.

I told him I was choosing to thank God no matter what place I finished.

Mike continued counting down, five, four, three, two...

He still didn't call me, and I knew my chances were over. I wasn't going to win. He called all the previous year's winners to the stage, then he said, "First place belongs to Diane Roark."

Take that Satan.

God overwhelmed me again.

I would be moving on to cook in the top ten in the dessert category. The love of God filled my heart and soul and encompassed every part of my being.

* * *

Texas Petite's Razzleberry pie filling was the infused ingredient everyone had to use for the third round of competition. I decided to make an elegant Strawberry Lemon Tart infused with the Razzleberry pie filling.

In previous years, I tried to accomplish too much in the third round. Knowing all the previous dessert winners were in the top ten pushed me to do more than I had planned. I admired each one of them and knew they were outstanding bakers. The top ten contestants included pastry chefs, bakery owners, and home cooks who sold their treats.

My Strawberry Lemon Tart was too ambitious. The tart was time-consuming, requiring slicing four pounds of strawberries and then arranging them in an elegant floral design. Strawberry slices were placed one by one with the pointed end facing out. I started the design with the first layer on the outer edge of the tart and worked my way into the center.

The strawberries had to be arranged on the large display tart plus ten four-inch tarts for the judges. We finished in the time allotted, but the sliced strawberries were too heavy for the lemon mousse, which didn't have enough time to firm underneath them. After taking the ten-inch tart out of the pan, a small portion of one side collapsed.

For World Food Standards, the display tart must look perfect. I knew I would get points deducted. Being a competitive perfectionist, it was a little disappointing.

I had to trust God. That's the recurring theme for me. In spite of my weaknesses, God still helped me to overcome them.

Appearances aside, the Strawberry Lemon Tart received high scores on taste, which gave me an overall finish in fourth place. The best news was that I had a golden ticket to compete again in 2020.

I had competed three times at the World Food Championships, and I was so grateful for the opportunity. God had overwhelmed me with three top-five finishes and two rare perfect scores against some of the best chefs, pastry chefs, bakery owners, and home cooks in the world.

"And he commanded the multitudes to sit down on the grass; and he took the five loaves, and the two fishes, and looking up to heaven, he blessed, and brake and gave the loaves to the disciples, and the disciples to the multitudes."
(Matthew 14:19 ASV)

God was multiplying my abilities and helping me to excel beyond my wildest expectations.

CHAPTER FIVE

FOURTH YEAR AT WFC

It's never too late to focus on your dreams.

2021 World Food Championships

The World Food Championships were canceled in November 2020 due to Covid. I thanked God that my golden ticket in 2019 was good for me to compete in 2021.

In that year, the World Food Championships' kitchen arena had a different setting. It was indoors at Fair Park in Dallas for the first time in WFC history. In previous years, the WFC kitchen arenas were outside, and we had to deal with the elements. Having a climate-controlled environment was going to be a game-changer when baking and make things easier for me.

Or so I thought.

I couldn't wait to see where I would be cooking. After registering, we were able to check out the kitchen arena.

The massive arena had at least fifty kitchens and I could feel the excitement building in the room already. The center of the arena had turn-in tables. Red carpet ran from the turn-in tables to the other kitchens directly opposite the first side. The red carpet was there to walk to where we turned in the finished dish. This added to the intrigue and made us as contestants feel a little like movie stars walking a red carpet.

Large banners were overhead. Each $100,000 winner since 2012 was on a banner. I imagined my name on one of them someday. For that to happen, I had to beat the forty to fifty contestants in the dessert category, then beat the nine other chefs who had beaten the forty to fifty contestants in their categories.

It's amazing how far I'd come. The first year I didn't think I belonged. Now I was dreaming of winning the whole thing.

Winning came with many perks. Many of these winners were now ambassadors for large brands and have been on Food Network and the Cooking Channel. Some even had their own shows. If I could somehow win, I was determined to use whatever platform God gave me to promote Him and to help others.

On the way to Dallas, Annie, my cousin and sous-chef, saw a billboard with Matthew 6:33 on it.

"But seek first God's Kingdom and his righteousness; and all these things will be given to you as well." (WEB)

That verse would be our theme throughout the completion. I thought about it continually. Leading up to the competition, I'd been consistently spending time with God each morning. The verse reminded me to hang on the promise to seek Him first and trust Him to give me the desires of my heart.

* * *

The first round was a whirlwind. With five minutes left to turn in my dessert, I heard voices all around me shouting, "Let's go!" Time was of the essence. Carly was screaming at me. One of her primary jobs was to make sure I was finished by the five-minute turn-in mark. The cake was heavy, and it might take a couple of minutes to walk it to the table.

Our Fourth of July cake included four layers of eight-inch cakes on the bottom. Caramel Apple Butter Coffee Syrup was added to each cake layer before filling with spiced fried apples, puff pastry pie crust, and salted pecans. The cake was frosted with maple caramel butter-cream and then dusted with hundred percent FDA-approved edible blue glitter.

A top cake floated above the four layers. Jerry had made me a cake stand with a steel rod through the middle of the bottom four-layer cake floating the top layer. The floating cake could only be added after bolting down the wood holding it up. The wood could only be bolted after the four-layer cake had been finished and threaded through the steel rod.

A time-consuming process. I had a plastic rod with rhinestones glued to it to slide over and cover the steel rod before adding the top board. After getting the floating cake on the stand, I noticed the rhinestone piece was on the table. Nothing we could do about it. We couldn't take everything off and add it. I didn't want to get disqualified for being late, and we were pushing the time limit.

Annie made an elegant red and white striped flag with modeling chocolate. It draped one side of the cake from top to bottom. The finishing touches consisted of a beautiful gold fondant rope around the bottom of the cake and a two-pound ceramic American bald eagle.

Not only was the cake heavy, but it was tall. Carrying it was a chore. The cake was about thirty-two inches high, which limited seeing directly in front of me. Thank God Marsha was right by my side. She guided me safely by telling me what was in front of me while I took tiny steps to the turn-in table.

After placing the cake on the turn-in table, and releasing my hands, I was overwhelmed with emotions. I couldn't believe we had accomplished such a huge task. With the help of my sous-chefs, Annie and Marsha. I couldn't have done it without them.

The round was sponsored by Weston Foods who provided the cakes. As we made our way back to the kitchen, I thanked God for his help and asked Him to help me get through another round. I knew I needed extraordinary strength since my lower back was hurting.

The kitchen was a mess, with glitter everywhere. We only had an hour to create our second round, Signature Dish. We tossed stuff in the trash and placed things on the floor to make room to work on our tart. The five minutes it took to make space for the second round threw me off.

Normally, after the second round, my two sous-chefs cleaned up the kitchen. They have always gotten supplies ready and organized while I turned the first round into the judges. Because the cake was so large, we needed a second tray of smaller cakes for the judges, plus someone to guide me safely to the turn-in table.

This put us behind from the beginning. The second round Caramel Apple Tarts were the worst looking apple tarts I'd ever made. My apple tart is normally stunning. Sliced apples form a beautiful rose completely covering the top of each tart. We had no time for that much detail. The apple roses didn't cover the entire surface of the tart like normal.

They were still pretty, but I was disappointed that the time had gotten the best of me again. Thankfully, the taste was not compromised, so I was still optimistic we would do well.

We made it to the top ten and ended up in sixth place. We would be moving on to compete in the next round. It also gave me a golden ticket to compete in 2022.

For the third round, I planned on making my Caramel Apple Tart again, but this time with the required Pyure Stevia, the sponsor ingredient. The tart had a layer of pastry cream or Crème Patissier using stevia and maple syrup. Maple syrup is a natural sweetener that didn't count against us. We could use a small percentage of sugar, but I had no idea how to calculate it. I decided to stick with the syrup. It went perfectly with apples and spices.

The thick, velvety custard was covered with elegant apple roses. On the plate and around the tart, I made a Crème Anglaise, a classic vanilla custard sauce. A Crème Anglaise includes simple ingredients, eggs, milk, heavy cream, sugar, and vanilla. It's all about tempering the eggs and the timing of the dessert sauce.

With the vanilla, I used stevia and maple syrup. In the Crème Anglaise, I added additional small apple roses to finish the dish. Making Crème Patissier and Crème Anglaise is my strength. I knew if we had enough time to form every apple rose, it would put me back into the top five, which had been a goal since finishing third in 2017.

While I worked on the Crème Pâtissier and Anglaise, Marsha and Annie tackled the tart shells. After putting the crust in the oven, they got busy on the apples. Annie was an apple slicing machine. It's easy to get a serious injury using a mandolin so she had to be careful. I had planned on slicing the apples, but Annie finished before me. I kept a watchful eye on her.

Marsha had been competing with me since the beginning. She's excellent at cooking apples and making stunning roses. By the time I finished the apple rose for the large display tart, she had finished making the roses for the five judges' dishes and the ones for the plates.

I was so thankful for them. The two ladies make up the best team I could have ever asked for.

The Apple Tarts were stunning. We had done our best, and it was up to God to do the rest. God had blown me away by allowing me to end up in the top five every time I competed. I had high hopes it would happen again.

We didn't have to clean the kitchen after making such a mess which I was also thankful for. SC Johnson was a sponsor and cleaned our station.

I could've used them at Floy's house a few weeks before when Marsha and I practiced our Fourth of July cake. The mess at our station brought back the memory.

A five-gram jar of Tinker Dust slipped out of Marsha's hands. The glitter hit the counter and exploded. It was like tossing sparkly flour into the air. A huge streak of super fine edible glitter covered an entire side of Marsha's face and down her body to the floor. It was on the counter, cabinets, baseboards, and cracks in the floor.

I managed to walk to the backdoor and opened it to let her out. We were both laughing so hard we could hardly stand up straight. I helped her slowly and carefully walk outside. Carly, my oldest daughter, a pediatrician, was standing on the patio. She was on the phone helping her cousin with her sick child. One look at Marsha and she was in stitches. I could hear uncontrollable cackling on the outside.

We all had a good laugh that day. Cleaning up was not fun though.

As we were leaving the kitchen arena after the third round, I ran back to grab a collapsible cooler that was left behind. Our kitchen number on the table caught my eye. I hadn't seen it before. Or at least it hadn't registered.

Number thirty-three.

During the first and second rounds, we were in kitchen number six.

Matthew 6:33. The billboard. Seek God first.

Were my kitchen numbers a coincidence? No, I don't believe so. God was telling me to keep seeking Him first, and He was going to give me the desires of my heart.

When I got back to my team, I told them about the numbers. Even if we didn't win that year, God was telling me to keep trying.

"I know one day we will make it to the final table if we keep putting God first in our daily life," I said to everyone. "It's a big dream, but it can be accomplished with goals and with God."

We moved up from sixth to fifth place in the dessert category, which gave me another top-five finish.

Four top five finishes in a row. My confidence was growing with each year of competition.

God is so good.

CHAPTER SIX

OVERCOMING CHILDHOOD HEARTACHES

I sensed a God who was looking out for me.

Mobile, AL

What will it be like at home today?

The same thought confronted me most days after school when the bus dropped me off in front of my house. The routine was excruciating too many days to count. My stomach would be in knots and my heart pounded as I reluctantly opened the front door.

I shared a room with my sister, Daisy. After putting my books on my bed, I'd cross the hallway and gently knock on the door and call out my mom's name.

When she was drunk, she didn't answer. Most of the time, I could smell the alcohol from the hallway. Red wine.

I always felt obligated to check on her but was terrified of what I might find on the other side of the door. Generally, she was lying on her bed. Passed out.

"Mom are you asleep?" I'd ask.

No answer usually.

My heart would be beating out of my chest.

The questions in my head were always the same. Was she dead? Unconscious? Sleeping? I'd tiptoe over to the side of the bed and say her name quietly. Sometimes, I gently touched her arm.

If she didn't answer, I'd repeat it a little louder, "Mom."

I had to make sure she was still alive. When she finally woke up and muttered something, I had mixed emotions. Thankful she wasn't dead, but the nightmare would continue.

More times than not, the sheets were soiled. If they were, I'd have already smelled it when I entered the room. It took all my self-control to keep from getting sick to my stomach.

On those days, I dutifully went around to the opposite side of the bed and took off the bottom sheet. I got some clean sheets from the linen closet and put the fitted sheet on that side, then went back to the other side and rolled her on top of the clean sheet. Next, I removed the nasty sheet and pulled the clean sheet to fit the other side. I tossed the smelly stuff in the washer.

Each time I changed her sheets, I promised myself I would never drink. Mom never realized I did that for her, or if she did, she never acknowledged it.

My mom hid her alcohol under my bed. Sometimes at night, she'd sneak in whenever everyone was asleep and get a bottle. Then take it back to the kitchen. I could hear the liquid hit the glass. The nights were hard because I couldn't go back to sleep. I pretended to be asleep, though, because I never wanted to confront her.

My mom's name was Mary. This went on for years. I never touched the alcohol nor said a word about it to my father or siblings. I was scared mom would get angry at me. Dad knew she had a drinking problem but had no clue she hid the spirits under my bed.

The drinking brought out the meanness in her. When she got mad, she would yell at me, and tell me I was a stupid liar. She tried to convince everyone, especially my dad, that I lied about everything. It seemed like every conversation ended with the words, "You'll never amount to anything."

Mom knew I wasn't a liar. She also knew that if Dad asked me, I'd tell him the truth. But her secret was safe with me. I wasn't going to tell Dad unless he asked. My fear was that my family would split apart, and I'd be the cause of it.

So, the dance in the darkness became the new normal. Mom hiding alcohol under my bed. Me changing her sheets when I got home from school.

I didn't realize that not telling anyone was making things worse. How could I? I was so young.

"He who conceals his sins doesn't prosper, but whoever confesses and renounces them finds mercy."
(Proverbs 28:13 WEB)

* * *

Looking back, I can see now how my mom's alcoholism affected my self-worth. It caused me to feel responsible for things that a young child should never have to deal with. Like taking care of her. Keeping her secrets.

Watching out for my little sister, Daisy.

One day, Daisy and I were riding bikes around our cul-de-sac. Daisy was five and I was eight. She was so excited to be riding a big-girl bike. She went around the cul-de-sac several times all by herself.

She'd yell at my brother and me to watch her. Then she'd look back to see if we were. One of those times, she took a tumble. Her head hit the curb. My oldest brother, Danny, ran to see if she was okay.

Daisy was limp and not answering. Danny picked her up in his arms and carried her toward the house. I ran right behind. Blood poured from the back of her head and ran down Danny's arm.

My heart did several somersaults in my chest. I feared the worst. Another thing my mother's drinking instilled in me. I was constantly afraid.

Then I felt guilty. I tried to protect my baby sister as much as possible, but I couldn't help but think that I had failed her this time. That this was somehow my fault.

Was she going to die? Was she seriously injured? Confronting these situations was so damaging to my young psyche.

By the time Danny got to the end of the driveway, Dad was there. They rushed Daisy to the hospital. She ended up having a severe concussion and received stitches where she busted her head open.

The whole time, I was at home, terrified. Not knowing how she was. I didn't find out that she was okay until dad came home. She had to spend the night at the hospital but would come home the next day.

That couldn't come soon enough. My Dad went to get her the next morning. When they got home, I heard the door open and raced to see her. Dad carried Daisy to the couch, and I was right beside him.

Daisy could have counted every tooth in my mouth from the massive grin on my face. It was one of the happiest days of my childhood after one of the worst days.

Dad said we needed to keep an eye on her, and he didn't have to tell me twice. I didn't leave my baby sister's side. I tucked a blanket around her lap, snuggled her doll in her arms, and crawled up beside her.

Daisy loved to talk, and I so desperately needed to hear her sweet voice. I had to turn my head to the side to wipe away the happy tears rolling down my face. I listened to every word she said. The more she talked, the more I realized she was going to be okay.

Even though I didn't know God at that point in my life, I sensed a God who had taken care of Daisy.

"A man of many companions may be ruined, but there is a friend who sticks closer than a brother." (Proverbs 18:24 WEB)

* * *

When I was eleven, my worst nightmare happened. My mom left with Daisy and Dale. She took everything we had and moved out of the house while my dad was at work and I was at school.

That evening, my dad sat my oldest brother and me down to have a talk.

"Where did they go?" I asked.

"I don't know," Dad said. "But it's going to be okay."

I wasn't so sure. Tears filled my eyes. Who would take care of Daisy and Dale? They had been my responsibility for as long as I could remember. Mom wasn't capable of taking care of them. Dale was ten, and Daisy was only eight. Too young to fend for themselves.

For months, I cried myself to sleep worrying about them. All I wanted was to have my brother and sister back with me. I could keep them safe. When Mom was drinking, they'd be neglected, and their lives would be in danger.

I felt so helpless and hopeless.

Later that fall, Mom returned home with Dale and Daisy, which was another day I will never forget. I actually saw them coming up the long driveway and raced out of the house. I couldn't wait for the car to stop. It finally did. When the car door opened and my brother and sister stepped out of the car, I gave them both a massive hug. I couldn't stop hugging them.

Dale and Daisy were home but so was mom. A mixed blessing. A powerful lesson for me to learn. Sometimes there was heartache and pain in the midst of joy.

Even though I still didn't know God at this point in my life, I sensed a God who was looking out for me and my brother and sister.

"The Lord hear thee in the day of trouble; the name of the God of Jacob defend thee." (Psalm 20:1 KJV)

By the fall of my ninth-grade year of high school, Mom was gone again. I was fourteen when she left home for good. My brothers were fifteen and thirteen, and my sister was eleven.

The school bus dropped us off at our house and, when we opened the front door, I immediately noticed that our green couch was missing. In fact, everything was gone.

At first, I thought maybe we were robbed. Then I assumed the worst. I scurried back to mom's bedroom and opened the door. She wasn't there, and neither was her bed. All her clothes were missing from the closet.

I went to the kitchen and opened all the cabinets only to find them empty.

My siblings and I looked at each other in disbelief. When dad got home, he was in shock. His face was red either in anger or embarrassment or both. He reassured us everything would be okay, but I wasn't sure.

I wondered how mom could leave four children and not say goodbye. How could she take all our food? What kind of woman leaves her kids and takes everything from them? Without even saying goodbye?

Someone who was very sick.

I didn't know at the time that God would never forsake me.

"When my father and my mother forsake me, then Jehovah will take me up." (Psalms 27:10 ASV)

* * *

When I was in the ninth grade, I was called to the principal's office. On the way, I saw my older brother, Danny. He was in the tenth grade and heading to the office as well. The principal met us at the door.

"You need to hurry to your mom's apartment," the principal said. "An ambulance is on the way to get her."

We'd never been to her apartment. Neither of us were sure where exactly she lived, although a relative had told us which complex. When we arrived, it wasn't hard to find her. The EMT's were putting our unconscious mom in the ambulance.

"What's going on?" my brother asked the policeman on the scene.

"Are you family?" he asked.

"Yes. We are her children."

He took us into mom's apartment where he showed us an empty pill bottle and an empty bottle of alcohol.

"It looks like she took these pills and swallowed them with alcohol," he explained. "The ambulance is taking her to the hospital. She must have called you first, and then us, before she lost consciousness."

Why would she call us?

We hadn't heard from her since the day she left. For months, I wondered if she was even alive.

They took mom to the hospital, and we never knew what happened to her after that.

* * *

My childhood wasn't all bad. There were many good memories. Even as a child growing up, I was fascinated with cooking. In some ways, it was an escape from my problems. It's where I found comfort and joy. By immersing myself in the process.

My dad was a major influence. When not frying catfish, hushpuppies, or having a shrimp, crawfish, or crab boil, from the fresh seafood we caught, he fixed a lot of rice and eggs.

They were his go-to staple. He fixed it often because we loved it so much. It was also inexpensive, easy to make, and filling. I passed the love of rice and eggs down to my family. Add country ham and cheese and you have my husband, Jerry's, favorite breakfast.

Here is my recipe:

Rice and Eggs

- 3/4 pound of Country ham, bacon, or sausage, chopped
- 2 TB of butter
- 2 cups of cooked rice
- Eight eggs
- 1/4 cup milk
- 1 cup shredded sharp cheese

1. Chop and fry the meat.
2. Remove the ham from the pan.
3. Add the butter.
4. Add the two cups of cooked rice.
5. Sauté it in the butter and ham drippings for 2 to 5 minutes.
6. Whisk eight eggs with 1/4 cup of milk and add it to the rice.
7. Cook and stir until mostly done, but still wet.
8. Add one cup of shredded Sharp Cheese on top of the eggs.
9. The dish is ready as soon as the cheese melts.

After Mom left, I found myself in the kitchen more and more and loved it. I made a lot of skillet meals at the time. Nothing fancy, but my daddy made me feel like they were something special and he was constantly affirming.

Raising four teenagers had to be hard on him, but he did the best he could and tried to fill the obvious void in our lives.

As I grew more comfortable in the kitchen, I prepared easy desserts. They weren't fancy either, but I thought they were tasty, especially for a teenager with no one to teach me, nor with any recipes.

Dad thought they were delicious. He raved about them, especially my coconut cake. His mom always made him a coconut cake from scratch for his birthday. My making it probably reminded him of a wonderful childhood memory.

Unfortunately, I never tasted any of my grandmother's coconut cakes, nor received her recipe. She passed away when my dad was fifteen, so I never met her.

One of the dishes I loved to make was fried chicken. My love of fried chicken came from my Aunt Dot. We would eat at her house most holidays and fried chicken and fixings were always on the table along with gumbo.

Little did I know how big fried chicken would be in my life.

The day after I turned sixteen, I walked a couple of miles to the closest place I could find to get a job. A fast-food chicken place.

"Do you have any openings?" I asked. "I live a couple of miles from here. Fried chicken is my favorite food, I'm a hard worker, and I would love to work here."

Ben, the man behind the counter, handed me an application. I sat in the dining room, filled it out, and handed it back to him.

I didn't realize Ben was the store manager. He looked at my application and asked me questions about my work experiences and when I could work. He also let me know the expectations he had from his employees.

Before I knew it, he wanted to know when I could start.

"Right away," I said enthusiastically.

Before leaving, he handed me some paperwork and a uniform. "Can you start this Saturday?" he asked.

"Yes, sir," I replied.

Before starting to work that Saturday, Ben sat me down, and went over my job description and company rules. When he got to the company policy of no dating other employees, a young man happened to be coming around the corner. He was covered in flour and had a tray full of breaded chicken. He was about to toss it in the hot oil.

Ben asked him to come and meet me. The boy put down the chicken and came to where we were sitting.

"Jerry, this is our new employee, Diane," he said. "Diane, this is Jerry. Jerry is a senior at Baker High School. We were just discussing employee dating. If you two decided to date, you better not let me find out about it."

Jerry had a smirk on his face but didn't say a word. I couldn't tell what he was thinking. I knew what I was thinking. I had no intention of breaking the rules.

"Yes, sir," I replied.

Over the next few weeks, I avoided Jerry as much as possible. He was cute, but I thought he had to be a lot older than me. I came to find out Jerry had skipped a year in school, which was why he was two grades ahead of me. He was only sixteen. Same age as me. He would be seventeen in March and graduating from high school in May.

Jerry didn't avoid me. He did everything he could to get me to go out with him. A couple of weeks after I started working, he asked me to go to church with him. I wasn't a christian, but I dreamed of a better life than what my alcoholic, dysfunctional mother had forced on me.

I turned him down. I wanted to go but was worried about the no-dating rule at work and what my father would say. My dad was strict. I'd never been on a date and didn't know how he would react. I figured Ben and my dad would consider going to church with Jerry a date.

Several more months went by, and Jerry kept asking. I did want to see what church was about. And Jerry was so nice to me, so hilarious, and so cute. I finally gave in and went to church with him. The first few times, I met him there so no one could consider it a date.

After church one Sunday, I had lunch with Jerry's mom, dad, and sister, Marsha. They all treated me like family. They were much different than my family. They seemed so loving and normal. I quickly fell in love with Jerry and his whole family.

How could I possibly know at that time that someday we'd be married?

Meeting Jerry at the chicken place was one of the best things that ever happened to me. One of the worst things that had ever happened to me took place there as well.

"Put your hands up and move back," the robber had said.

I remember it like it was yesterday.

I was at the chicken place. It was closing time. When the man entered the restaurant, I was the only one working the front counter. It was Friday night, and I was actually getting ready to go home. We had no customers in the restaurant, so I got an early jump on my cleaning duties.

I was standing with my back toward the counter cleaning part of the warming racks where we put the chicken. When I heard the front door open, I glanced at the clock hanging on the dining room wall. It was a couple of minutes before closing. I put down my cleaning stuff and turned around to see if I could help the customer. The man was a few feet from the counter.

A gun was pointing at my head.

He said, "Slowly open the register."

My body started to shake uncontrollably, especially my hands. I was doing my best to get the register open but kept hitting the wrong button. Each time I hit the wrong button the cash register made dinging noises. Because I was so nervous, I had forgotten how to open it.

The gunman grew impatient. He kept fidgeting around. Looking at the door to see if anyone was coming. Then back at me. Giving me threatening looks. Waving the gun in my face.

It seemed like forever, but finally, the money drawer flew open. He said, "Put your hands up and step back."

I quickly obeyed.

The robber reached over the counter and into the register. He snatched the money while I stood in panic and shock. As he was grabbing the money, another co-worker appeared from the back. I wanted to warn her, but it was too late. She saw the man and let out a shriek.

The man moved the gun back and forth between the two of us. He told us to get under the counter. I dropped to my knees and hurried to do what he said. I got under the counter directly under the cash register. My co-worker did the same at the other end of the counter about six feet away.

I heard his footsteps as he walked toward the front door. As he was leaving, he said he would shoot us if we got up.

I still didn't think we were out of the woods. The whole time I thought I was going to die. I remember thinking that a bullet could go through the counter and hit me if he decided to shoot me anyway.

So, I crouched under the counter and covered my head. He left, but I still didn't move.

I found out later that my co-worker, who was under the other end of the counter, had gone to the back and had the store manager call

911. I still remained under the counter frozen in fear. The manager tried to get me to get up.

I told him that I would get up when the police arrived. I was still afraid that the robber would return.

Finally, the police arrived. I was still hiding under the counter. He told me it was okay to get up. He even reached out his hand and helped me up. I was never so happy to see an officer.

After giving me a chance to catch my breath, he asked me several questions. I told him everything I could remember while it was fresh on my mind.

"Did you get a good look at him?" he asked. "How tall was the man? How much did he weigh? What did the gun look like? What did he say? What happened?"

After retelling everything I could remember, the policeman asked the same questions to my co-worker.

A few days later, they had a suspect in custody. The police called the store manager, Ben, and asked all of us to go downtown to the police station to pick the suspect out of a lineup. The policeman even offered to pick me up if I needed a ride.

I asked Ben if I had to go. He nodded yes.

I did need a ride. I'd never driven downtown by myself and wasn't sure I could even find it. I was terrible at directions and scared to death to see the robber.

The policeman did come to get me. He opened the back door of the police car for me to get in it. I was the victim, but I felt like a criminal. I was thankful for the ride, though, but I thought I never wanted to ride in the back of a police car again. I imagined everyone we passed wondered what I did wrong.

Once we reached the police station, I followed the policeman down a long hallway with a large glass window at the end of it. The policeman explained that a line of possible suspects would enter the room when I was ready. They'd line up along the back wall. He would tell them to slowly turn to the right and then slowly turn to the left so I could get a good look at each one.

"Take your time and look everyone over," the officer said. "They can't see you. This window is one-way glass."

I took a deep breath. The policeman asked if I was ready. I nodded yes.

"Send them in," he said. As soon as the robber walked in, I recognized him.

The policeman must've seen the recognition on my face because he immediately said, "Do you see him?"

"Yes, sir."

"Are you sure?"

I looked at everyone again and nodded.

"It's the person on the far left," I said.

He spoke into his handheld device, "We're finished."

He took me to a room and talked with me for a minute. He said, "We have witnesses that picked out the same man. We believe he also robbed the grocery store behind where you work, plus a gas station. When we caught this man, Gus, he had lots of drugs stuffed in his underwear."

He told me I'd receive a court summons in the mail and that I'd have to testify. He could see fear in my eyes, and I'm pretty sure my whole body started shaking again. The officer said it would be okay. He thanked me for coming and called another officer to take me back to work.

A few months later, I received the court summons. It was my first time being in a courtroom, and I was nervous. I didn't want the robber to see me. I was worried he would later come after me. Since he was identified as the one who robbed several other places, including a grocery store, and a gas station, several witnesses were there. They began by calling witnesses one at a time from the grocery store. Next, they called the witnesses from the gas station.

When they got to the fried chicken restaurant where I worked, he called for a witness. My co-worker was called to the stand first. She was sworn in and began to tell her story. After she finished, I knew they were going to call me next.

By that time, my legs were trembling. My plan was not to look at Gus, who was sitting in the front row. To my surprise they didn't call me. After my co-worker's testimony, the judge said the court was over.

Honestly, I was too young and naive to know what was going on. At sixteen years old, I was the youngest one in the courtroom. I believe the lawyer must've heard I was having a hard time and didn't want to call me to the stand unless necessary.

A few months later, I received a letter stating Gus pled guilty to all the robbery charges. He was sentenced to twenty years in the state penitentiary. The letter also said I would be notified when he was released.

At the time, I didn't know God but now know He was protecting me by not requiring me to testify. He also provided Don, Jerry's father, to help comfort me. He happened to be a witness in a different case but in the same courtroom.

His case was scheduled right after mine. When Don entered the courtroom, he spotted me and made his way to sit down by my side. I was surprised to see him but extremely grateful.

For years, I asked God why I had to experience being robbed. Years later, while lifting my hands to God, and begging him for answers to a different problem, He answered me. He reminded me of the time when Gus pointed a gun at my head and told me to raise my hands.

The Holy Spirit whispered to me, *You don't have to raise your hands to God as you did with the robber, but you have a choice to surrender all your problems to Him.*

He gave me a clear picture of how He will take care of me when I surrender my difficulties and trust Him to take care of them. I understood for the first time that not only is God with me during difficult times, but He can turn my horrible experience into something meaningful if I will love and trust Him.

I no longer question why I experienced a gun to my head. Now, I know it's a reminder to surrender everything to God and trust Him to take care of it. To me, trusting God with the big things in life is much easier than trusting God with the daily things in life.

From that experience, I witnessed God's protection and Him working so many things out in my life.

God is a big God and can handle all my problems.

If I hadn't worked at the chicken place, I wouldn't have had a gun to my head. I also might've not met Jerry. My husband. My soulmate.

Sometimes, we just have to let God work out the good through the bad.

CHAPTER SEVEN

HEARTACHES TO LOVE

The greatest of these is Love.

There have been two defining moments in my life. Competing and winning at the World Food Championships have been highlights, but not defining. Meeting Jerry and Jesus are the two most important things that have ever happened to me.

Even though I was thrilled to meet Jerry, I wasn't so sure my dad would be. My daddy's sisters, Aunt Dot and Aunt Doris, told me stories about how my granddad would sit on the porch with his shotgun in his hands when their dates arrived. He would stare at the frightened boys without saying a word.

Jerry meeting my dad was similar. Only without the shotgun. Although, if looks could kill, Jerry would've been dead ten times over. Jerry came to my house to pick me up for our first initial date. The door slammed, and I came running to the front door. I expected to see Jerry standing in the entryway.

He wasn't there.

"Is Jerry here?" I asked.

"Yes, he's at the door," my dad said.

My heart sank to the bottom of my chest. My dad hadn't even invited him into the house. He just slammed the door in his face.

Embarrassed, I quickly opened the door and invited Jerry inside and officially introduced him to my dad. My dad didn't crack a smile or say a word to Jerry. He refused to shake his hand even though Jerry reached out to shake his.

I reminded Dad of where we were going, and he reminded me what time I was to be home. Jerry and I got out of there as quickly as we could.

While I suspected my dating would be difficult for my dad, I had no idea it would be this hard.

It took several years, but dad eventually came around. Before Jerry and I married, and especially before dad's death, they became good friends. Knowing my dad approved and they got along was a good thing because I was madly in love with Jerry. I loved my daddy too and would've been grieved if the two most important men in my life didn't like each other.

What's not to love about Jerry?

He has a crazy side to him that always makes me laugh. Back then, and continuing to this day, he's constantly doing silly things. He has a quick wit and keeps me in stitches with his singing and dancing. He's also intelligent, handsome, and loves God.

Our first date was one of the best days of my short life to that point. Going to church together made it special. Sundays became the highlight of my week over the next few months.

Growing up, we didn't go to church. Before meeting Jerry, I'd only been to church a couple of times with my cousins. Going to church was something I needed, but also getting to know Jerry and his loving family were doing wonders for my well-being.

Several weeks later, I had a surprise for Jerry. One I knew was going to make him extremely happy.

"Jerry, can you meet me at church?" I had asked.

"Sure," he said. But why?"

"I asked God to come into my heart, and I want to be baptized now."

I'd been studying the Bible with a lady at the church. One day, I made up my mind to accept Jesus as my Savior and be baptized.

The baptism was at University Church in Mobile, Alabama. Jerry, Floy, Don, and Marsha along with Marshall, the preacher, were there. I was so excited to start my new life as a Christian and knowing my sins were forgiven. I had a new identity in Christ. That was important for me since my identity to that point had been shaped and molded by my mother who told me I'd never amount to anything.

Something I refused to believe from that point on.

"Therefore if any man be in Christ, he is a new creature:
old things are passed away; behold, all things are become new."
(2 Corinthians 5:17 KJV)

I felt God watching over me many times as a child. Now, I knew there was a God who loved me. He sent his Son, Jesus, to die for me, and I knew I would see Him in heaven where He was preparing a place for me.

Things from my childhood started to make sense. I saw them in a different light.

When I was about ten years old, I had a dream. In it, an angel appeared and said, "I am watching over you." The words were clear as day and the angel floated over my bed wearing white. When I woke up and sat up, the vision was gone. I had no clue who he was or what he meant, but I thought about it for years.

Life was so difficult growing up with an alcoholic, but this dream was comforting to me even at ten years old. I often found myself looking up to heaven and wondering if someone was watching over me.

Now I knew there was. After accepting Jesus as my Savior, I had no doubt God had been watching over me.

Six days later, May 28, 1983, I graduated from high school.

I had a new heart, a new boyfriend, a degree, and a new beginning in life. I couldn't wait to see what the future held for me.

"Brothers, my heart's desire and prayer to God for them is that they may be saved." (Romans 10:1 NIV)

"For God so loved the world, that he gave his only begotten Son, that whosoever believeth in him should not perish, but have everlasting life." (John 3:16 KJV)

* * *

My wedding day

As I gathered my wedding dress and loaded the car with all the things I needed for the day, I couldn't help but be a little sad. I thought about the people I loved who wouldn't be at my wedding including several cousins, aunts, uncles, and even my mom. Due to years of generational family dysfunction, the wedding was not all it should've or could've been.

After arriving at the church early, I parked my car several blocks away in the neighborhood across from the church.

They'll never find my car this far from the church, I thought.

It was a new car, and I didn't want anyone to "decorate" it. Of course, that didn't work out too well.

The day was also hot. In Mobile, Alabama, or LA, as I call it for Lower Alabama, the temperature and humidity in August can be brutal. I arrived at the church around noon, sweating like a pig. I'd already done my hair and makeup and was beginning to regret it. My hair was a frizzy mess and the makeup streaked down my face like I'd been crying.

When I noticed a broken fingernail, I did start crying, completely ruining what was left of my makeup. I'd gone to great lengths to look perfect for the most anticipated day of my life, and it wasn't starting out well.

My emotions were swirling around inside of me like a tornado on the plains.

In retrospect, I wasn't crying because of the broken fingernail or the ruined makeup. Those could be fixed. I was crying over what couldn't be fixed.

The loss.

Knowing my mom wouldn't be there on my special day. Growing up without a mother left a huge void in my life. My dad did his best to fill it, but how could he?

The emotions were mixed. I was angry at her for not being there and sad at the same time. If I wasn't careful, these painful memories could ruin my big day.

After crying a minute, I looked around at the empty church auditorium and started to pray, "Lord, please help me get through this day. Thank you for Jerry who introduced me to you and my new family who is faithful to you. Help me to love and support Jerry for the rest of my life. Please let our marriage last forever and never let divorce enter our hearts. Let me break the chain of dysfunction and addictions in my family. Let my children and grandchildren follow you all their life. Bless my life with Jerry. In Jesus's Name, Amen."

Once I began to focus on who would be there, rather than who wouldn't, I felt better. Thank God my siblings were there, and my daddy was able to walk me down the aisle.

And of course, Jerry would be excitedly waiting at the end of the aisle to marry me. What a blessing the day would be if I embraced all the wonderful things I had in my life.

Somehow, we pulled everything together and the time came for me to walk the aisle. As the music played, I grabbed my daddy by the arm. He leaned over and asked, "Are you okay?"

I was on the verge of tears again. This time, happy tears.

I kissed him on his cheek, and said, "Yes, I'm ready. Thank you for never leaving us."

As we walked down the aisle, I couldn't take my eyes off Jerry. He had a massive grin on his face. At that moment, I forgot about everything except getting married to him. The man I loved with all my heart. I knew he had a heart for God, and we were going to build a wonderful life together.

> "And if it seem evil unto you to serve the Lord, choose you this day whom ye will serve; whether the gods which your fathers served that were on the other side of the flood, or the gods of the Amorites, in whose land ye dwell: but as for me and my house, we will serve the Lord." (Joshua 24:15 KJV)

And that's what we've done. Built a wonderful life together. Keeping our vows to each other, and serving the Lord, striving every day to have a household that serves the Lord.

Jerry filled a void in my life that only a wonderful husband can fill. That didn't mean the heartache left by my mom was gone.

* * *

Time to forgive

For years after we were married, mom was constantly on my mind. She had caused so many problems in our family. I hated her for leaving our family. For the drinking, taking pills, yelling at us, saying I would never amount to anything, never supporting me at any school functions or homework, robbing me of having friends over, losing out on my childhood, and all the other heartaches I experienced growing up.

I carried around this bitterness for a long time.

One day, I reached out to an older cousin on my mom's side. She told me some stories about our mother's childhood. A light bulb went off in my head. For the first time, I understood mom was hurting due to all the extreme trauma she faced as a child. I realized her bad experiences were taken out on me and my siblings.

That revelation changed everything.

I'd prayed for this generational curse to be stopped and that I wouldn't pass it on to my kids. At that point, I realized it was up to me. Forgiveness was a big part of breaking the dysfunctional chain.

Time to forgive her for everything.

Up to that point, I'd never really forgiven her. Refusing to let God's forgiveness flow through me left a heavy weight of anxiety I no longer wanted.

I wanted my children to have a much better life. It wasn't enough to just teach them the word of God. They needed to see the power of it in me. Giving God my hatred towards my mom helped me find peace in the dysfunctional chaos of childhood.

I started praying daily for mom to know there is a God who loves her.

I could do nothing to change the bad memories from my childhood, but I was going to choose how the experiences changed me. I decided to use the memories as a reminder to be more understanding to everyone.

This is a good lesson to always keep in mind as you deal with imperfect people. You never know what may trigger others to behave the way they do. I no longer wanted to judge my mom when I hadn't walked in her shoes.

More telling was the revelation that if I didn't choose to forgive, it would likely change me into the angry, bitter person who would repeat the generational problems or curse on to my children.

Forgiveness was not for my mom's benefit. Forgiveness was about trusting God with the good, bad, and ugly to create something beautiful out of my life.

I was thankful for my cousin sharing information with me about our mom's past. I was able to forgive my mom. The process also made me better able to understand others and to forgive them, not knowing what they'd been through that caused them to hurt or offend me.

"And we know that all things work together for good to them that love God, to them who are called according to his purpose." (Romans 8:28 KJV)

Letting go of the past allowed me to embrace the plans God has for my life.

"Do not judge, and you will not be judged. Do not condemn, and you will not be condemned. Forgive, and you will be forgiven. (Luke 6:37 NIV)

* * *

More unexpected heartache

Resolving one heartache, didn't mean another wasn't right around the corner.

The phone rang early in the morning. I picked it up and heard the voice of my oldest brother, Danny.

"Diane," Danny said. "Dad is gone!" Shocking me to my core.

He passed away in the middle of the night. Danny had just stopped by to check on him when he found him. Daddy was only fifty-eight. Even though he wasn't in the best of health, I didn't know he was going to die.

I burst into tears. Between sobs I told my brother we'd be there as soon as we could.

I'd just seen daddy the Friday before. We'd gone home to see my father-in-law, Don's, retirement ceremony. He retired at forty-four years old from the U.S. Coast Guard after twenty-seven years of service. While there, we visited daddy before heading home to Montgomery.

Because Dad was weak from kidney failure, he was in a wheelchair. We had a nice visit, but I could tell he wasn't feeling well. When we got ready to go home, he insisted on following us to our car in his wheelchair. As I got into the car, my dad had said, "I want you to know I picked out a cemetery plot."

"You're not leaving me," I said. "You're way too young."

"One day I will," he said, "and I don't want you to worry about what to do with me."

While driving home, I told Jerry, "It was as if he knew he was going to pass away soon. Danny said when he found dad, he had his hand on his Bible. He must've been praying and reading it. I think it's God's way of letting me know we will see him again one day in heaven."

Jerry said, "I agree, I think having his Bible open was a sign he was getting right with God. Remember that. It will help you get through this difficult time."

I have thought about daddy's Bible being open many times over the years. I hang on to the thought of seeing my dad one day in heaven.

> "Let not your heart be troubled: ye believe in God, believe also in me. In my Father's house are many mansions: if it were not so, I would have told you. I go to prepare a place for you. And if I go and prepare a place for you, I will come again, and receive you unto myself; that where I am, there ye may be also." (John 14: 1-3 KJV)

Jesus said in this world we'd have many troubles. Heartaches. Daddy dying was one of the most difficult ones I've faced. I know that I've had more than most to deal with, but less than many others. I'm not the first person whose father has died. Obviously.

It's not the heartaches that define us. It's how we handle them. Knowing Jesus has made all the difference. I'm not sure how I would've dealt with them all without him. I remember how hard it was to live with the pain before I accepted Christ as my Savior. It's still difficult sometimes.

After Jesus said we'd have many troubles, He said that we are not to worry, because He has overcome them all.

That's the promise I hold on to.

I have Christ who helps me, and I have Jerry to go through them with me. I hope you get that message in this chapter. The stories are not to share my heartaches and to have a "Woe is me" pity party. They are to share how I've been able to overcome them with God's help and with a wonderful husband by my side every step of the way.

CHAPTER EIGHT
STARTING OUR FAMILY

You are stronger than you think.

Jerry and I were married but had little money. We both worked and went to college at the same time. We were determined to finish our degrees before starting a family.

It wasn't easy.

I had a full-time office job, plus a part-time job at a jewelry store while taking as many hours of classes as I could. If I accomplished the goal of graduating from college, I'd be the first person in my immediate family, and only the second in my extended family to receive a degree.

I wanted so much for my father to see me graduate. That drive propelled me forward. My father never gave up on us. He worked several jobs to make ends meet and never complained about it. Without his sacrifice, I never would've had the opportunity to go to college to begin with. I couldn't let him down.

Jerry had a part-time job and drove from Mobile to Gautier, Mississippi, every day to finish a degree in radiology technology. He went to night school, and also served in the Army National Guard. His National Guard training as a medic helped him complete his degree early.

It took seven years, but we both finally had our degrees. What a joyous moment that was in our household. More of a relief than anything else, but something of which we were extremely proud.

In February 1985, Jerry was offered a job in Montgomery, Alabama.

At first, I wasn't sure. I'd never been north of Mobile. I hated to leave my family, but it was an excellent opportunity for Jerry, and we decided to take it. We packed up everything we had in a small U-Haul and headed to Montgomery to start a new season of our life together.

"And above all these things put on love, which is the bond of perfectness." (Colossians 3:14 ASV)

After we were settled in Montgomery, I said to Jerry, "We have our degrees. You know what that means."

"What?" he asked.

"We said once we had our degrees, we were going to start a family."

I had a wide smile on my face when I said it. His reaction would tell me if he was as ready as I was. When he started grinning from ear to ear, he made me the happiest woman in the world at that moment.

We were naïve in thinking we could just decide when we wanted to have children. That once we decided, it'd automatically happen right away. Months passed and I still wasn't pregnant.

What followed was a series of tests and fertility treatments that allowed me to finally conceive.

"You're having a baby girl," the ultrasound technologist said.

I was so excited, I rushed to the hospital where Jerry was working to tell him the news and show him the ultrasound pictures.

"What are we going to name her?" he asked.

I suggested Carly, after my dad.

"Baby Carly, sounds perfect."

That settled it. Our firstborn, Carly, was born perfectly healthy and brought happiness to our family immediately. I was so thankful God allowed me to have a sweet baby girl. I only wished my father had gotten to meet her. He'd have been thrilled that she bore his name.

> "It is of the Lord's mercies that we are not consumed, be-
> cause his compassions fail not. They are new every morn-
> ing: great is thy faithfulness. The Lord is my portion, saith
> my soul; therefore will I hope in him. The Lord is good
> unto them that wait for him, to the soul that seeketh him.
> It is good that a man should both hope and quietly wait
> for the salvation of the Lord."
> (Lamentations 3:22-26 KJV)

My maternity leave lasted six weeks. A sitter was arranged to watch Carly while I was at work. Melinda was a good friend from church and was a blessing to us. Even then, the first day I had to drop her off with Melinda was painful. I didn't want to leave Carly. Tears streamed down my face when I pulled into Melinda's driveway.

I wanted to stay home with her and had prayed that God would help us find a way for me to stay home with our sweet baby girl. I waited a long time to have her, and I wanted to enjoy every minute before she grew up. Which I knew would happen fast.

After dropping Carly off that first day, I went to work. Everyone was happy to see me, but I felt guilty for leaving my baby. I wanted to be a full-time mom more than anything. I'm sure my upbringing was bringing out the range of emotions. I grew up mostly without a mother. I wanted to give Carly the love I never received from my mom. Most of all, I wanted my baby to know I would never leave her.

But I had a full-time career. Jerry and I had sacrificed a lot for me to get a college degree. We also needed the money. As much as I loved the work, my heart was with my daughter. I desperately wanted to be home with her.

Several months later, Jerry came home from work with a serious look on his face.

"Diane," he said, "I've been offered a medical sales job in Atlanta. I know you don't like big cities, but we would only have to live there until I finish my training."

I was confused. It sounded like a good opportunity, but how could we upend our entire family and move out of state? So many questions flooded my mind. Where would we live? Where would I work? Who would watch Carly while I was at work?

Even more disconcerting was that Jerry would be gone most of the time.

"You'll be in Atlanta by yourself for weeks at a time until I finish training," he explained. "I will have to commute between New York and Atlanta every other month for a year."

What? A year?

That seemed like an eternity. Not only were we moving to a new city, but I'd have to make the transition without my husband there to help me. I felt overwhelmed. I didn't want to do it.

Until I realized it was an answer to my prayers.

"Do you think I'll be able to find a job in Atlanta?" I asked Jerry.

"Honey," Jerry said, "the new job will pay enough money that you won't have to work."

Those words caused my heart to leap with joy. This was what I wanted. To stay home with Carly.

But in Atlanta?

Such a drastic move was daunting. So many things would have to come together. Selling our house was one major obstacle. It wouldn't be easy to sell right away. I thought of a thousand reasons why we shouldn't move. But Jerry wanted to and I would do almost anything to quit work and stay home with our daughter.

I was still growing as a Christian. Learning to trust God to work out the details was new to me. We put our house on the market. To my surprise, it sold right away. I was so thankful to God for that blessing.

More confirmation that God was behind the move. That didn't mean everything would be easy. The move certainly wasn't. Living in Atlanta was harder than I even imagined it would be. I had no idea that trusting God to sell my house was a piece of cake, (pun intended), compared to the challenges we would face in Atlanta.

My faith would be stretched to its limit. The Bible says that God will not put more on us than what we can stand.

That principle was put to the test in Georgia.

* * *

Atlanta to Macon. The road to a miracle.

We were only in our new home in Atlanta a couple of days before Jerry was off to New York to begin his training. As soon as he left, I felt incredibly lonely. I was a stay-at-home mom but felt like a single mom for months. Over the coming weeks, Jerry was gone most of the time.

What was I thinking when I agreed to move to Atlanta?

So many things made me want to go back home. Kind of like the children of Israel who prayed for God to deliver them. Once he did and they were in the desert, they wanted to go back. I had a lot to learn about trusting God.

Jerry was right about me not liking big cities. I was in a massive city for the first time and didn't know a soul. To make matters worse,

I had a terrible sense of direction and was afraid to venture out even to find the grocery store.

At least I had Carly. I don't think I could've gotten through it without her. Carly and I ventured out and found a church. There I was able to find some encouragement and support and Carly was able to find some playmates and be exposed to spiritual things at an early age. I didn't have that growing up and was determined that my kids would know God.

In the midst of the struggles, I had a sense God was taking care of us. It was a tremendous lesson to learn. I'd prayed God would let me be a stay-at-home mom. This wasn't how I would've planned it when I voiced the prayer. But we don't always get to do things our way.

All I could do was make the best of it and realize it would only be temporary. Eventually, Jerry finished his training and received a full-time job offer covering Central and South Georgia. We moved to Macon to be centrally located in his territory.

When Carly was two, Jerry's job was busier than ever. He spent four nights a week on the road. I wanted to have another baby, but it didn't seem like a good idea. And Jerry was gone all the time. I was raising Carly mostly by myself.

Did I want to bring another child into that situation?

In addition, I'd had a hard time with my first pregnancy, and the doctors weren't sure I'd be able to have another child. Would fertility drugs work a second time? There was no guarantee. My first pregnancy was hard. Did I even want to go through that again?

So, Jerry and I talked about adopting. We both had a heart for all kids to have a loving family and learn how much God loves them. However, the more we prayed about adopting, we realized the timing wasn't right. We decided to wait until Jerry could get a job where he would not have to travel as often.

Baking filled a huge void in my life during that time. Carly and I baked goodies and used them to meet our neighbors in Macon. Carly was a big fan of strawberries. We often made homemade strawberry cupcakes with a strawberry buttercream, which everyone loved.

How could I possibly know at the time that strawberry cake would be the first thing that came to mind when thinking about the infused ingredient at World Food Championships? In 2018, I used Walmart's Rosé to make a Strawberry Rosé cake with a Strawberry Rosé Buttercream.

I probably would've never competed in the World Food Championships without those days in Macon with Carly perfecting cooking with strawberries. As hard as those times were, I can look back and see how God was with me through it all.

> "Don't you be afraid, for I am with you. Don't be dismayed, for I am your God. I will strengthen you. Yes, I will help you. Yes, I will uphold you with the right hand of my righteousness." Isaiah 41:10 WEB

***

The faith of a child

One day, Carly came to me and said, "Mom, we're having twins. I asked God for them."

She was four years old. I could hardly believe the words coming out of her mouth.

"What are you talking about?" I asked.

"I asked God for twins," she said confidently. "One to hold each end of my jump rope. Since daddy's always gone, I need someone to hold the other end of my jump rope."

I didn't even know she knew what twins were or how she could've come up with something so out of the blue for such a small child.

I didn't want her to get her hopes up. "Carly, I had a hard time getting pregnant with you," I said. "I'm not sure we can have any more children."

At that point, I'd resigned myself to the fact that I wouldn't be able to have more children on my own. Much less twins. But Carly was insistent. She prayed at every meal and every night before bed that I'd have twins.

A couple of months later, I felt like something was wrong with me. I went to the doctor for a yearly check-up and told him some of the symptoms I was feeling. When he told me I was pregnant, I almost fell off the patient table.

I told the doctor how my little daughter had been praying for me to get pregnant, but I didn't think I could.

"It looks like God answered her prayers," he said. "You are very pregnant."

"Carly said God told her I was going to have twins."

He dutifully nodded but had no comment. What were the odds of having twins? Slim to none. Twins didn't run in either of our families.

"We need to do an ultrasound," the doctor said. "I think you're far enough along to run the test."

"Can my husband and daughter come into the room with me?" I asked.

He said they could, and we were led to a room where the technician performed the ultrasound. A few minutes later, the doctor came in and looked at the screen. He twisted his lips to the side, looked at me, then at Carly. Something was up. I think I knew what it was but didn't know how in the world it was possible.

He bent down to where Carly was standing and said, "You were right, little girl. You're going to have two more babies in your family."

I almost fell off the table a second time.

Carly answered quickly and with a wide grin, "I know! I prayed for them." Like she never doubted it for a minute. She probably didn't.

The doctor replied, "Your prayers were answered."

Tears formed in my eyes as I was overwhelmed with emotions. God cared enough about my daughter to answer her prayers. It also warmed my heart that my daughter had so much faith even at an early age. A lot more faith than I had in that situation. I never in a million years believed I was going to have twins.

Lord, give me the faith of a child, I thought. *Help me to always pray with boldness.*

Jerry and I looked at each other in amazement. We both knew the truth. It had to be a miracle from God.

> "And said, "Most certainly I tell you, unless you turn and become as little children, you will in no way enter into the Kingdom of Heaven." (Matthew 18:3 WEB)

CHAPTER NINE

OVERCOMING THE HEARTACHE OF A TRAUMATIC BIRTH

The struggle you're in today develops strength for tomorrow.

By the time we arrived at the hospital, the twins were ready to be delivered. For a while it looked like they wanted to be born in the parking lot of the hospital. The pregnancy had been extremely difficult. I had no idea how difficult things were about to become.

"I can't make it to the hospital," I cried out to Jerry. I was already in labor. He had rushed me to the hospital immediately when I started labor, but it still didn't seem like I'd be able to make it inside before the babies were born.

How could I deliver two babies on the sidewalk?

"Please go get some help," I said. "I'll wait here."

He hesitated. "Diane, I can't leave you. We don't have much further to go. Can you take a few more steps?"

"Jerry, if I try, I'm afraid the boys are going to fall out of me."

We'd learned from the ultrasound that I was going to have twin boys. The oldest would be named Casey, and the youngest Caleb.

It looked like these two were going to start giving me trouble from the get-go.

Jerry finally agreed and ran off to get help.

While he was gone, I prayed, "God, please help me. I need your help. Lord, please don't let me give birth out here on the street." I'd barely finished my prayer when Jerry and a nurse rushed out of the emergency room with a wheelchair.

Casey was literally born minutes later.

Caleb didn't follow right away. He was born breach which created immediate complications. Once he was finally birthed, he had to be rushed into intensive care.

For a long time, we didn't know what was wrong with him. It took several hours before the doctor came to update us on his condition. Caleb had bleeding on the brain. At first, the doctor didn't seem that concerned. He assured us that everything would be okay. But I had a gut feeling they were wrong. Call it a mother's instinct. Because of the difficult pregnancy and even more difficult birth, I feared the worst.

Little did I know my worst fears were nothing compared to what my baby would have to endure over the coming weeks and months.

Casey had to stay at the hospital for a few days for observation. When the extent of Caleb's problems became clearer, the prognosis wasn't good. He was looking at months, not weeks in the hospital. If he were ever able to come home. The doctors couldn't provide any assurances.

Expecting twins, I'd prepared myself for the fact that our morning routine would be upended. I had no idea it would turn into an ongoing nightmare. A bad dream that never ended. Like the movie *Groundhog Day*. I kept living the same day over and over again.

Each morning began with tears. They flowed uncontrollably as I had to leave Casey and go to the hospital to be with Caleb. Casey only weighed four pounds. He needed his mother. If Caleb didn't need me even more, I don't think I would've been able to leave him.

Carly needed me as well. The only real time I had with her was when I dropped her off at kindergarten every morning. This was one of the hardest things for me. Carly and I had been together twenty-four hours a day, seven days a week for all of her first five years. I missed her terribly. I missed the times we baked together. When we took our goods to the neighbors. When Carly was in preschool, we made home-made cupcakes together for her class parties.

Cake had always been Carly's favorite and she loved baking cakes with me. I had been her room mom at preschool, and we made Carly's favorite dessert often. Now I couldn't volunteer at her school. I couldn't bake with her. I barely had the mental or emotional energy to be there to put her to bed at night.

All that concern I had about Carly growing up without a mother was happening. Beyond my control, but I still felt the guilt. What could I do? My baby was dying and needed his mother.

On the days I could drive Carly to school, I tried to fill the void with her. But she always wanted to talk about her brother. What could I say? She was mature for her age, but I couldn't tell her all the details. All I could really tell her was to keep praying and trust God to take care of Caleb.

I reminded Carly that she had asked God for the twins and God had answered her prayers. We had to believe He didn't give Caleb to us only to take him away.

On her own, Carly asked her teacher and class to pray for her brother. I've always been amazed at her sensitivity to the things of God.

Caleb's condition worsened by the day. His neurosurgeon said that they were having trouble stopping the bleeding in his brain. Most of the time, the brain can absorb the blood, but his couldn't. From August 28th to September 20th, Caleb's head continued to fill with blood and swell. On September 20th, Caleb had a CT-Scan, which showed a Grade 4 bleed, the worst brain bleed possible.

The neurosurgeon explained, "The blood in Caleb's head is blocking his spinal fluid and keeping it from draining. He has hydrocephalus. Caleb needs a shunt to drain the fluid out of the affected ventricle of the brain and into the abdominal cavity."

I was quickly becoming proficient in medical terms. A shunt is a small plastic long tube, something like a straw, but much longer. When the spinal fluid builds up, his head swells and causes extreme headaches. The doctor said surgery was required but came with risks.

Shunt complications can occur during or weeks after the procedure, including excessive bleeding from breaking more blood vessels and infection. Other common complications with shunts include obstruction and over-draining of cerebrospinal fluid. Any of these issues can lead to excessive pressure from spinal fluid building up causing horrible headaches, nausea, and vomiting.

The coming days were touch and go as the surgery didn't work like we had hoped. Caleb was in a lot of pain and his head began to fill with even more blood and fluid. His shunt was working but not well enough to drain everything. Caleb started having seizures. They gave him phenobarbital for seizures and morphine for his extreme pain.

I insisted on staying by his side, even at night. That left me with no time for Casey or Carly. Their care fell completely on Jerry and his mother, Floy. She stayed at our house at night, which allowed me to stay with Caleb and hold him through the night.

I barely slept. The bible verse to pray without ceasing was something I was beginning to understand firsthand.

Caleb's breaths were shallow. He was in constant pain. As was I, although my pain was emotional. It broke my heart to see my baby like that, when all I could do was comfort him. Only God was there to comfort me in those dark and lonely nights.

Caleb was hooked up to all kinds of machines. One night, alarms went off. A crew of medical staff were in the room in seconds. They grabbed Caleb from my arms and started C.P.R. Caleb was in cardiac arrest. All I could do was watch helplessly as they worked frantically to bring him back to life.

I begged God not to take him.

They quickly got him stabilized and placed him back in his isolette. It was better that I didn't hold him, so I pulled up a chair and held his hand the entire night. I begged God to heal him.

Then, out of the blue, it happened again. The alarms sounded. My heart was racing. Anxiety pulsed through me like water from a fireman's hose. The staff was back in the room within seconds.

They saved his life again. How much of this could my son take? What about me? Everytime the alarm sounded, it sent me into a panic. The roller coaster of emotions had fried my nerves like a defective electrical socket.

Caleb made it through the night, but he was clearly not doing well. He looked pale and lifeless. The next day the doctor's words were no comfort. "Caleb lost too much blood during the surgery. He needs a transfusion.

After the neurosurgeon left, I fell to my knees and cried out to the Lord. "Lord, are you there? Please help Caleb."

We had an answer to prayer. God heard my cry. Jerry was able to give Caleb blood. After the transfusion, Caleb's body became very cold, and he was placed under warmers. Things stabilized for a short period of time.

Two weeks after his first shunt surgery, Caleb had emergency surgery. His CT had shown his shunt had failed. His head started to fill with more fluid and blood than his head could contain. This caused extreme headaches. Caleb obviously couldn't verbalize how much pain he was in, but I could tell. A mother knows what her child is going through.

The doctor said a new complication had arisen. There was too much blood in Caleb's brain to be drained with a shunt. He suggested a rare procedure. To brainwash Caleb—literally. The surgeon washed his brain with a 2-liter bottle of saline. Instead of replacing his shunt, he gave him an external drain.

The external drain acted as a shunt. It drained the spinal fluid and blood from Caleb's head to a bag hanging on a pole. He kept assuring me that Caleb was going to be okay. Eventually. They just had to get the blood out before placing another internal shunt back in his brain.

Two days after his second shunt replacement, Caleb developed a staph infection in his brain, which was a risk of surgery and having an external drain.

Why did we keep going from one complication to another?

We'd solve one problem and another one developed. When would it all end?

I continued to pray fervently. I wasn't angry with God, but I didn't understand why my prayers weren't being answered. I couldn't see it at the time, but they really were. Caleb's condition was dire. It'd be a miracle if he survived. In retrospect, the fact he was still alive was a miracle and an answer to prayer.

At one point, I began to lose hope. I was past the point of exhaustion and each medical emergency drained the faith from me.

Caleb would need a powerful IV antibiotic for weeks to kill the staph infection. Four weeks after his first blood transfusion and two weeks after his staph infection, he needed another blood transfusion. Jerry couldn't give blood since it'd only been a few weeks since he last did so. This time his grandpa, Jerry's dad, Don, gave Caleb blood. After the transfusion, Caleb's body temperature fell extremely low again, so he was placed under a warmer a second time.

By this time, I was barely functioning from all the pressure. Jerry insisted that I start coming home in the afternoons to get a break from it all. At first, I was resistant. Caleb needed me. After praying about it, I knew Jerry was right. I couldn't spend every moment at the hospital. My family at home needed me, too.

It seemed unfair that I was forced between choosing which of my children to help. It had to be done. At that pace, my health was beginning to suffer.

Saying goodbye to Caleb in the afternoons was extremely difficult, especially when he was having one of his terrible days. The NICU nurses would assure me he was in good hands. I would kiss him goodbye and head to school to pick up Carly.

Jerry, Floy, and Don would visit Caleb in the afternoons and evenings while I spent time with Carly and Casey. It never failed. Every day around five o'clock in the afternoon, Casey would start to wail. He had colic and it was impossible to soothe his bellyaches. He would scream for hours. I felt terrible because I couldn't help him.

I did my best to console him, but nothing helped. I just held him close and rocked him each evening while listening to him cry.

As we rocked back and forth, I would cry out loud to God, begging him to help Casey and Caleb. To help all of us. I knew my God was a big God who had answered so many previous prayers, including giving us twins. I had to trust He was going to make everything better. It seemed like my prayers usually worked. Eventually, Casey would fall asleep.

This routine went on for months. The pressure on our family was almost unbearable.

To make matters worse, Caleb wasn't getting any better. In fact, his condition was getting worse. Every day, my hopes would sink a little further into the quicksand of despair.

One of the worst parts of it all was watching Caleb suffer. Most mornings, lab technicians tried to get blood from Caleb. His blood and the spinal fluid had to be clear of infection before the neurosurgeon could replace the external drain with a new shunt. Caleb had a PICC line to draw the daily blood but getting it from the line was not an option most days.

It often didn't work, and the lab had to draw blood by sticking him with a needle. They eventually replaced his PICC line, but they still drew some lab work by pricking his heels. This was not an easy task. They would squeeze and squeeze, but nothing would come out. He rarely had even a drop of blood to give.

Caleb would scream in pain from the needles. My heart broke anew every day.

How much longer could he endure this?

I was exhausted beyond belief, but I barely thought about myself. Whatever I was going through was nothing compared to the suffering my baby was experiencing.

By this time, Caleb was old enough to look into my eyes. I could see the pain and the fear. I could feel him pleading with me to make it all stop. He couldn't possibly understand why all these people were hurting him. How could he know they were trying to save his life?

Was his life worth saving if this was going to be the quality of it?

Finally, I reached a point where I couldn't take the heartache any-more. Caleb had a horrible night, and the next morning, the lab was having an even worse than usual challenging time getting blood. After the lab tech left, I leaned over Caleb who was still screaming. I put his precious head in my hands. While sobbing, I prayed, "Heavenly Father, Caleb nor I can handle any more pain, heartache, or disappointments. God, you are the only one who can help us. I have been begging you to help me. I don't know what else to do. If it's your will, please let Caleb quickly improve and not suffer so much pain. I know you know he has been in constant pain since his birth."

I tried to catch my breath as I could barely get the words out between the sobs.

"Heavenly Father, please heal Caleb or take him to heaven if he has to suffer. My heart can't bear seeing him scream for help when no one can help him. Nor can he take any more severe headaches from shunt failures and shunt infections. I know you watched your Son suffer on the cross, and you know the heartache I'm feeling. I know you have a plan and a purpose for my sweet baby boy. Let your will be done and not mine. In Jesus's name. Amen."

After praying and holding Caleb's precious face, he fell asleep. At that moment, I felt a breakthrough. I had given Caleb and all his medical problems entirely to God. I thought I had before, but maybe not. I knew then that I had. My son was in God's hands.

I had faith that God loved Caleb more than I did. I had confidence He was going to help us. I left the hospital that day with a sense of peace that I hadn't felt in weeks. The kind of peace you feel when watching a sunrise come up over the ocean on a beautiful day.

It was a peace I can't fully explain. But I knew both Caleb and I would be okay no matter what happened. Within days, Caleb had surgery to remove the external drain and get a new shunt. The surgery went well, and he was moved from intensive care about nine weeks after his birth.

Several days later, the doctor gave us wonderful news. Caleb could go home.

November 1st, 1996.

I was ecstatic. My faith was bolstered. Although, my faith wasn't dependent on my circumstances. If Caleb's condition had worsened, I would've still been at peace. Saddened, but determined. I was going to trust God no matter what.

I gained from that experience a faith stronger than anything I could've ever manufactured on my own. As I began to trust God more, I was given emotional resources I didn't have before.

Before being released from the hospital, the neurosurgeon came to see Caleb. They had set up an appointment for him at Vanderbilt in Nashville on the following Monday with his new neurosurgeon. He gave me a stack of CT scans of his head and shunt x-ray series to give to his new doctor.

Caleb had over a hundred CT scans and x-rays during the first few months of his life, and they weighed a ton. Dr. Robert flipped the latest one up on the view box while trying to explain to me about the damaged areas of Caleb's brain.

He said, "Due to excessive blood and spinal fluid in his brain, Caleb has brain damage."

I looked at him and said, "I prayed that if God let him live, He would take care of him."

"Your son is going to live."

Those words brought an unspeakable joy to my heart. Whatever damage Caleb had to his brain, we'd learn to live with it, with God's help.

I reassured Dr. Robert that everything was going to be okay. Usually, the doctor was the one trying to reassure the parent. I wanted him to know that God had this.

After the doctor told me his brain damage was in his ventricles and frontal right lobe, I asked him if he thought Caleb would ever walk.

Dr. Robert said, "I can't answer that question. He has a lot of damage. But the brain can heal, especially in infants."

I thanked the doctor for everything he had done, and we took Caleb home for the first time.

Not the home where we lived when Caleb was first born.

While pregnant with the twins, Jerry and I decided it was time for him to get a job with less travel. Jerry got a job offer with the same company in Tennessee. The new job would be less travel. We jumped at the opportunity without even praying about it first. We put our house on the market in Macon and couldn't wait to move.

The house sold right away. The movers arrived on October 31st to load up our furniture and deliver it to our new home in Tennessee on November 1st.

Caleb came home on the same day.

Our drive to our new home in Columbia, Tennessee, was about five-and-a-half hours. I was so excited to have Caleb out of the hospital but trembled inside. I kept praying and asking God to take my fears and calm my nerves on the way to Tennessee. At the same time, the devil filled my thoughts. Testing my faith.

What if Caleb stopped breathing on the drive?

The enemy reminded me of all Caleb's shunt failures, infections, and surgeries I had witnessed over the past few months. There was a battle in my thoughts that was driving me crazy. I could feel the inside of my body trembling. I had told the neurosurgeon Caleb was going to be okay, but did I really believe it?

Now I wasn't sure.

We hadn't been in the car for an hour when it became dark due to a horrible thunderstorm. The lightning popped all around us. The thunder sounded like it was inside the car. The rain beat on the roof relentlessly. It seemed to last the entire drive to Columbia. It was not easy to see the lines on the street, the taillights from the car in front of us, or the street signs.

A storm was also brewing inside of me as well.

How could I take care of my baby? I wasn't a nurse. What if he needed emergency care? CPR? I knew how to do it, but could I revive Caleb in the car if he went into cardiac arrest?

My thoughts were out of control.

Floy was driving. Jerry was driving our furniture in the moving van. I had no idea how Floy was able to drive through the torrential downpour. I prayed God would guide her to Tennessee. I was so thankful she was able to help us and knew I couldn't make the trip without her.

I was in the back of the van with Casey on one side and Caleb on the other. Caleb cried most of the way. I didn't know why. Casey cried too, still suffering from colic.

I was so afraid Caleb was crying because his shunt was failing. I worked hard to feed, talk to, distract, play with, pray, and even sing to them with little success. Just like the storm, the crying went on for hours.

I felt helpless. I was failing my babies, especially Caleb. A fear of Caleb dying on our way to Tennessee overwhelmed me.

Eventually Casey finally fell asleep, and Caleb stopped crying but the fear didn't go away. Nor the feelings of inadequacy. Or the guilt.

In the hospital, I had promised Caleb that when he came home, I would never let him cry continuously. No matter how hard I tried, I couldn't keep that promise.

I felt I was letting God down. I felt like a horrible mother.

The faith had abandoned me like my mother had abandoned us as kids. I was physically there for my kids now, but what if I couldn't give them what they needed? The stress around me was causing me to doubt. I was crumbling under the pressure of the storm and getting my babies safely to our new home.

Carly sat in the middle seat and helped her Grammy read the road signs. She had been reading since her second birthday. She read the road signs and tried to be helpful. Unfortunately, due to the downpour, Floy ended up missing a turn. Because of the wrong turn and the horrible rain, and stopping to change diapers and use the restrooms, the five-and-a-half-hour drive was closer to an eight-hour trip.

We were all exhausted when we finally pulled into the driveway of our new home.

As soon as we did, I felt a release. A strong sense of relief. God had gotten us there safely. Caleb was still alive. None of my worst fears had come to pass. In fact, they'd been for nothing. A waste of valuable mental and emotional energy.

I suddenly felt bad for doubting.

I thanked God that we made it safely but felt guilty for having had so much unbelief. How was I going to face what lay ahead if my faith was so weak?

I've heard it said that the battle with the enemy is in the mind. It was so true that day. I wished I'd done better, but all I could do was keep trying moving forward.

When I got into my new house, I felt better. For the first time, our entire family was together.

Jerry's cousins from the Nashville area had spent the day with him and Gramps unpacking our boxes and setting up our house. They had everything unboxed and organized by the time we arrived.

When I walked into the new home, which I had never seen before, I was home. My new home was the refuge I needed from the storms that had been pounding me for months. When everyone left, I put Carly and the boys to bed and crawled into my bed. I began sobbing out of overwhelming gratitude for God answering my prayers even though I had doubted Him.

I knew once again He worked everything out in His timing.

I felt my faith returning.

"Yahweh is good, a stronghold in the day of trouble; and he knows those who take refuge in him." (Nahum 1:7 WEB)

They say difficult circumstances help to build faith. I can say with certainty that's true. I didn't know it at the time, but my faith would be tested again. In ways I hadn't thought possible.

And sooner than I was ready to face it.

CHAPTER TEN

ALCOHOLISM AND MEDICAL BILLS

Be positive, patient, and persistent.

The pressure was mounting.

When it seemed like we'd somehow managed to survive one trauma, another one reared its ugly head. Soon after moving to Columbia, my husband, Jerry, admitted he had a drinking problem.

Caleb's extended hospital stay had made things difficult for everyone. Combined with the move to Columbia and the pressure of his new job, Jerry had turned to alcohol to cope. Prior to the move, I'd spent almost every waking minute in the hospital with Caleb and hadn't realized how big a problem it had become.

Jerry drank as a teenager but promised he would never drink after we were married. Alcohol was a problem in his family as well, and he assured me he'd never let it become a problem in our family. Given our family histories, a problem was a real possibility.

I had seen Jerry's heart for God and believed he would never drink. So, it came as a shock when I discovered the extent of the problem.

I was devastated. I felt betrayed and overwhelmed. It seemed like the pressure was too much to bear. Growing up with an alcoholic mom made me hate alcohol. I knew firsthand how it could destroy a family. I promised myself I would never drink nor marry an alcoholic.

How could Jerry do this to me? Knowing my history.

But what could I do?

I had two babies to feed every two hours. One with a shunt keeping him alive. Caleb now suffered from cerebral palsy and seizures. The medical bills were piling up. We were trying to adjust to a new environment, away from church, family, and friends. As if that weren't enough, Carly had her own set of problems as a young girl to manage.

What if I had to face those problems alone? I couldn't live with an alcoholic again. That wasn't an option. But how could I deal with all those other things as a single mother?

Thankfully, Jerry agreed to enroll in an outpatient treatment program at the local hospital. That came with its own set of problems. How did I know if the program would work? I didn't. It also meant more medical bills and Jerry had to be gone for extended hours when I needed him at home.

To add further pressure, moving to Columbia had turned out to be a mistake. We thought we were doing the best thing for our family since Jerry would be home all the time. Shortly after moving there, Jerry's company reorganized the territories. He went from covering a third of Tennessee, to covering the entire state, which meant he was back on the road four days a week.

With him gone more than half the time, I was lonely, and all the care of the kids fell on me.

Also, how did I know if I could trust him to stay sober on the road?

During those dark times, I found myself doing the only thing I knew to do. Trust God.

The answers to my prayers started coming in almost right away.

* * *

Caleb's problems didn't give me time to wallow in any self-pity anyway.

Moving to Columbia meant he had to start all over with a new doctor. Dr. Robert had been his doctor since birth. Dr. Tulipan came highly recommended, and Vanderbilt was a great hospital. We met him on Monday, November 4, 1996, for an initial evaluation and an opportunity for Dr. Tulipan to become familiar with Caleb's case.

Dr. Tulipan was concerned about the size of Caleb's head. It should have grown six to eight cm but had only grown one cm. Other than that, things looked good. As good as they could, considering the circumstances. Which was encouraging. The most immediate concern was a shunt failure.

A week later Caleb started throwing up. We took him to Vanderbilt's emergency room. One of the main signs of shunt failure is vomiting and headaches. Dr. Tulipan ordered a CT scan before we even arrived at the ER.

I never assumed the worst. Instead, kept believing God that Caleb was going to be okay.

The CT looked good, and the vomiting wasn't a result of a shunt failure. Dr. Tulipan said Caleb had a virus. That was a relief. The bad thing about it was that the virus circulated through our entire family making everyone miserable for a few days.

Dr. Tulipan wanted to see Caleb in a month to run another CT scan. Again, everything looked good. Caleb's shunt was working, and his head had started to grow.

I told the doctor I'd been praying for Caleb through every challenging situation and believed with all my heart that God was going to take care of our son. God had answered our prayers back in Macon. I had to believe He allowed Caleb to live for a reason and wasn't going to take him from us in Tennessee.

That faith kept propelling me forward even when we'd get bad news. Even when the doctor would express concern, or Caleb would have a setback and had seizures.

Even when Jerry admitted his problem with alcohol.

Somehow, I knew God was going to get us through it.

At the beginning of the new year, Caleb had an EEG that didn't show seizure activity which meant we could slowly wean him off phenobarbital. Getting off this strong seizure medicine was great news. The medication made him seem like a zombie.

It also meant Caleb was making progress.

I was thankful for every small victory.

Around that time, Caleb's medical bills really started to pour in. I began a pile on the desk which kept growing almost daily.

Talk about trusting God. At one point, I added up over a million dollars in hospital and doctor bills!

Insurance paid some, but we were still waiting to see if they would pay a portion of the others. Even then, how could we possibly pay all of the amount left over? Jerry could work ten jobs over ten lifetimes, and we'd never be able to pay all those bills.

Rather than let the bills sit in the pile as a constant reminder of the futility, I prayed and asked God what to do. He told me to pay what we could and let Him take care of the rest.

At His direction, I called every single one of those bills and explained our plight to them. Every insurance company, doctor, hospital, lab, and emergency room received a call from me. Before each call, I said this prayer, "Lord, you know we have no money to pay all this debt. Please provide us with as much help as possible with these bills."

God blessed each phone call and significantly lowered our debt. To the point where it was manageable. Miraculously, we were able to pay off the remaining debt in a few years. It strained our budget, but thank God I loved to cook and started cooking all our meals at home. I learned how to prepare budget-friendly meals.

Eating at home had many added benefits. The dining room table grew to be a special time for our family. It was a relaxing place to communicate. We not only ate together but talked, cried, shared memories, played games, and laughed together.

We celebrated birthdays and holidays at that table. Jerry and I taught our children family values, family history, manners, and most importantly God's Word around that table. During breakfast, Jerry would read a short devotional. As the kids got older and had busy schedules, we made it a priority to continue eating together.

Jerry gained control over the problem with alcohol, which was another huge answer to prayer. Our family was able to stay together. I'm so thankful to God for that.

And also to Jerry.

Things could've gone a different direction. He was able to do something my mom was never able to do. Overcome the problem with alcohol. He did it for me. For our kids. For himself.

It made all the difference in the world. I know I would've survived had the outcome been different. I'm just so thankful it wasn't.

At the time of this writing, we're coming up on thirty-eight years of marriage.

* * *

Glenn and Fran

Jerry and I believed we never should've moved to Columbia. We didn't pray about it beforehand and made the decision out of our own thinking without really seeking God's will.

I learned valuable lessons from that. Things always work out better if you pray about them first. But I also learned that even when we make a mistake in life, it doesn't mean God abandons us.

A lot of good things came out of our time in Columbia. When you ask God for help, you never know where that help might come from.

Glenn and Fran were a retired couple who lived directly across the street from us.

Fran was a former nurse. What a godsend she was. She loved coming over at bath time and helping me bathe the boys and get them dressed. She often helped get the boys ready for church. Carly enjoyed playing cards with Fran while I got chores and dinner done.

Mr. Glenn helped me overcome many stressful situations. With Jerry gone a lot of the time, Glenn was a grandfatherly figure for the boys and also handy around the house when something broke, or I needed a strong hand.

One such situation comes to mind. When the twins were a few months old, I dropped Carly off at school and went to the grocery store with the boys. When I got home, I unlocked the house and returned to the car to fetch the kids and the groceries. I grabbed Casey's car seat handle over one arm and Caleb's seat handle over the other and headed back to the house.

I pushed the door all the way open with my foot and placed Casey's car seat next to the open door. I put Caleb's car seat to the left of the door on the floor, leaving me a space to walk in the middle.

I returned to the car to retrieve the groceries. When I got back to the door, it was closed.

Strange.

After setting the groceries on the ground, I tried to open the door. It was locked!

I looked through the glass and saw Casey had scooted halfway out of his car seat and was screaming. He must have accidentally kicked the door closed, and I had no idea how it locked.

Jerry was out of town, so I ran across the street to get Glenn. He came quickly to check out the situation and decided we needed to break the glass in the door to get the door opened.

He found something in the garage to break the glass in the door. That didn't seem like a good idea. What if the shattered glass hit the boys?

I remembered asking God to keep the boys safe.

Glenn decided breaking the glass wasn't a good idea and went back in the garage. There he found something to cut the glass rather than breaking it. The glass popped out and didn't shatter.

God had answered my prayer. My babies were safe.

Unfortunately, I would need to call for Glenn for help several more times during the few years we lived across the street. At nine-months-old, Casey started walking and locked himself in the bathroom.

It seemed like Casey had a knack for locking doors!

Glenn always came to my rescue. It seemed like Jerry was always out of town when Casey was up to his antics.

I was so grateful for God blessing me with this special retired couple who helped me over and over.

Why would I mention these stories? Everybody has little annoyances in their lives they have to deal with. I've had my share, along with the big problems such as alcoholism and medical emergencies. I'm not the first person to deal with an alcoholic family member or a special needs child.

That's not the point of the stories. I share these to convey a greater message. We all need God to deal with the troubles in life. He's always there for us. Ready to help, if we will let Him.

"For I am persuaded that neither death, nor life, nor angels, nor principalities, nor things present, nor things to come, nor powers, nor height, nor depth, nor any other created thing will be able to separate us from God's love which is in Christ Jesus our Lord." (Romans 8:38-39 WEB)

I'm thankful to Glenn and Fran. They were one of God's many blessings to us.

Glenn loved banana pudding and I loved making it for him. I made Glenn his favorite dessert as much as possible. It was a small way of showing them how grateful I was for their help.

It's said that the troubles in life prepare you for dealing with life. How could I possibly know that meeting Glenn and Fran would help prepare me years later for the National Banana Pudding Festival?

CHAPTER ELEVEN

BANANA PUDDING FESTIVAL FINALIST

If you never try, you'll never know.

My heart raced as I opened the email.

It was from the *National Banana Pudding Festival* held yearly in Centerville, Tennessee. Centerville is a small town of around 3500 people, but the festival draws a crowd. Thousands of people go to River Park every year to watch the national banana pudding cook-off, to enjoy live music, crafts, and the Puddin' Path. More about that later.

Banana Pudding is my family's favorite dessert and something I feel comfortable preparing. For more than thirty years, I've made it for every holiday and special occasion. If there were a contest tailor made for me, banana pudding would be it.

The festival was slated for October 2017. You had to be picked to participate. I sent in my recipe with high hopes I'd be selected. Ten people were invited to cook live in front of an audience.

I opened the email with anticipation pulsing through my veins.

Congratulations, you made it into the top ten! You will be cooking live at the National Banana Pudding contest.

DIANE ROARK

I threw my fist up and said "Yes" before I could even finish reading the email. The correspondence went on to say when, where, and what time the contest would be. It also told me what I needed to bring and who to check in with before the contest.

Jerry was working in his office and came into the kitchen to see what all the commotion was about. I told him the good news.

"I'll be cooking live at the Banana Pudding Contest in Centerville, Tennessee."

He grabbed me in a bear hug and spun me around. "I had no doubt. What are the dates? I'll find us a place to stay."

I couldn't wait to call Marsha, my sister-in-law and sous chef at the World Food Championships.

"Marsha, I made it to the top ten at the Banana Pudding Festival," I said.

"Awesome! Can I go and cheer you on?" she asked.

"Absolutely! I wish I could have a sous chef, and you could be by my side."

"I'm excited for you and can't wait to watch."

That is Marsha. She's always so supportive.

When we arrived at the festival, the place was abuzz with activity. The craft vendors were already setting up. To the left of the stage, food trucks were lining up. The food sounded delicious, and I couldn't wait until they opened.

The festival had a huge area with kid games and rides. To the right of the stage was a large tent for the Puddin' Path. The patrons could pay eight dollars to taste ten different puddings made by local non-profits. The Banana Pudding Festival started in 2010 as a fundraiser for local charities supporting victims of disasters, fires, tornadoes, and floods. It was so successful it became a yearly event.

The stage was in the center of the festival. In front of the stage was a pavilion with chairs. Five kitchens were set up on the stage. A table was located at the front of each kitchen. While working on their banana pudding, the contestants faced the audience. Each table had a bright yellow tablecloth. Bananas and Nilla Wafers were sitting on the table.

Nilla Wafers was a sponsor. No surprise there. I'd already expected it.

Behind each table was a stove. After looking around the festival, I couldn't wait to get started. The excitement was building inside of me. I knew my recipe well and was confident it would be a hit, and that I would finish on time.

After checking in, I received my station information and assignment to cook in the first round. Since they had ten contestants but only five kitchens, they would have two rounds of cooking. I was not only cooking in the first round but at the first station. For some reason, I felt an added pressure being number one. The first kitchen was to the left of the stage and the closest to the activities at the festival. I had seen pictures of a previous banana pudding contest. The crowd builds there if they can't find a seat under the pavilion.

At the appointed time, we were called to the stage. I took a deep breath and entered from the side stairs. As soon as I got to the top of the stage, I was in my kitchen. Jerry was right behind me. He was pulling a large cooler with all my ingredients.

After finding a place for the cooler and thanking Jerry, I looked out to see the chairs filling up. Caleb, Carly, Marsha, and Floy were all there to cheer me on. After giving them a quick wave, I got busy setting up my supplies.

My banana pudding began with homemade pastry cream or custard using half & half, sugar, vanilla, eggs, and cornstarch. Over the years, I have made custard many times. A lot can go wrong when making pastry cream, but I was confident I could fix it. I made an original banana pudding recipe by layering the homemade custard with Salted Caramel and Rolo's. It also included the traditional sliced bananas and vanilla wafers. It was a hit with my family, and I was counting on the judges liking it as well.

The countdown began.

5, 4, 3, 2, 1. Start!

I began cooking. The first thing I did was heat my milk and sugar on the stove until it began to steam but not boil. In a separate bowl, I whisked together my egg yolks, salt, and cornstarch. I used twelve egg yolks because I tripled the recipe. I needed enough pudding to fill both containers.

A four-quart pudding trifle dish was for the judges, and the additional pudding was for those who purchased a ticket to taste. A two-quart pudding was used to auction off and raise money for local charities.

I heated my half & half with half the sugar until steaming. After whisking my egg yolks, salt, and cornstarch until thick and pale, I tempered my eggs. I drizzled about a cup of the warm milk into the eggs while whisking and then added the rest of the hot milk into the eggs without worrying that the eggs would curdle or scramble.

While continually whisking, I cooked the mixture over a medium heat until thick. I finished my custard with pure vanilla and butter for shine. Here is the recipe:

- 4 egg yolks
- 1/4 cup cornstarch
- 1/8 teaspoon salt
- 2 cups half & half
- 1 cup sugar

- 1 tablespoon pure vanilla paste
- 2 tablespoons butter.

I quickly put the hot custard into a rectangle container. The 9 x 13 dish gave me more surface space for the custard to cool faster. When finished, I put it into the cooler, to cool and continue thickening.

I had about forty minutes remaining.

I started working on the caramel, unwrapping the Rolo's, slicing the bananas, opening the Nilla Wafers, and whipping heavy cream. I was ready to layer the pudding but waited until the last ten minutes. I knew this would cut the time close, but the custard was hot. It needed as much time as possible to cool.

They announced we had ten minutes to finish cooking.

I grabbed the custard and started layering all my ingredients. It was not the consistency I was hoping for. The pudding thickens as it cools. It needed to be cooled a couple of hours before layering it.

I continued layering the pudding anyway and finished on time.

The banana pudding looked beautiful in the trifle bowl I brought for the judging. We were given handmade pottery "Puddin' Pot" for the second pudding to be auctioned. The festival organizers gave each contestant a "Puddin' Pot" too. It had the words, Banana Pudding Festival 2017, on it. The "Puddin' Pot" was perfect to remember the festival.

A number of tables were set up in front of the stage. We were to decorate our section of the table and place our pudding on the table. My display of fall items was colorful, and my pudding looked fabulous. After the second round of contestants finished their banana puddings, the judges were going to pick up a sample of each contestant's pudding. They would take it back to their judge's tent.

When the first judge started coming through for a sample, I was the first stop. I couldn't get all the layers on the dipping spoon. I had so much homemade whipped cream, Rolos, bananas, caramel, and Nilla Wafers on top that I missed giving the first judge the pudding.

We had small four-ounce cups to fill. One spoonful filled the cups. When filling the cup for the second judge, I dug for the custard. It was a hot mess. October in Tennessee wasn't ideal for cooking outside. Sitting in the heat, it had thinned out.

After the judges, we served the line of people who paid to sample the ten finalist's dishes. It was time to auction our second bowl of banana pudding. I said a few words about the ingredients in my dish and how I made it before the auctioneer began. It took me back to when I was in school, and people chose teams for kickball.

Until I was picked, I would think I wasn't good enough, and no one would choose me. I had the same feeling standing on the stage, watching people bid on my banana pudding. I was concerned no one would start the bidding. Once the first person started and other bidders jumped in to bid, relief washed over me. I was excited about my banana pudding helping to raise over $200 for the amazing nonprofits.

After the auction, we made our way to the main stage at the festival. A band was playing for the crowd. Shortly after arriving, the banana pudding finalist went on stage. They called the fourth to tenth person in random order and handed us a beautiful gift basket.

We never found out what place we finished. I was a little disappointed being the competitive person I am. They only announced the first, second, and third place winners. Since I didn't win, it was probably better I didn't know.

While I didn't finish in the top three, I was thankful for having the opportunity to compete in the National Banana Pudding Contest and couldn't wait to enter again the next year.

* * *

Year Two

The following year, I entered the National Banana Pudding contest again. This time I entered with a no-cook banana pudding called Turtle Banana Pudding. It was thickened with cream cheese and didn't need to be chilled as much. I layered the pudding with homemade candied pecans, caramel, turtle candies, Nilla wafers, and bananas in a 9 x 13 dish. That size of dish allowed for thinner layers. I was able to reach every ingredient in one scoop. This allowed me to get all the layers for the judges to taste.

After checking in, I received my station information and assignment to cook in the first round. For the second straight year, not only was I cooking in the first round, but I was in the first station. Kitchen A.

That's the winning station this year, I thought.

I was actually pleased since I was familiar with that kitchen. This year, I wasn't nervous at all. I entered the stage from the stairs on the side of the stage and hurried to get everything set up. I wanted to visit my competitors. I knew several of them from competing at the World Food Championships. They were not just my competitors but friends. We have a lot in common with loving this crazy competitive competition of Food Sport.

From the stage, I could see Jerry, Caleb, and Carly. Plus, my mother-in-law, Floy, Marsha, and my husband's cousin, Dennis, who had come to cheer me on. I was excited to see them and humbled to know they drove hours to be there.

Another countdown and we were off.

In a large bowl, I added two eight-ounce packages of cream cheese. Using an electric hand mixer, I beat the cream cheese until smooth and creamy. I blended in two fourteen-ounce cans of sweetened condensed milk and continued beating in four cups of milk and two large boxes of instant vanilla pudding, along with two teaspoons of pure vanilla, and one teaspoon of banana extract until combined and then placed in the cooler.

In a large skillet on low, I added a stick of butter, a tablespoon of sugar, one teaspoon of salt, and two cups of chopped pecans. Once melted, I combined everything, including two cups of chopped pecans. The pecans were pressed down on the bottom of the skillet and cooked pecans over low heat until lightly browned. Once they browned and smelled amazing, I spread them out on a large baking sheet to cool.

While doing this, a banana pudding judge came around to ask me what I was doing. I answered his question and handed him a warm, sweet, and salty pecan. I was thrilled when he said it was delicious.

I whipped two cups of heavy cream with a half cup of confectioners' sugar to decorate the top of the pudding. The pudding and heavy whipped cream were enough to fill the two-quart "Puddin' Pot" and a 9 x 13 dish.

I sliced the bananas and removed the pudding from the cooler to fold two sixteen ounces of frozen whipped topping into it. Next, I layered my Turtle Banana Pudding.

- Half of the pudding on the bottom of the 9 x 13 baking dish.
- Half of the box wafers on top of the pudding.
- Sliced bananas to completely cover the wafers.
- Drizzle the bananas with salted caramel and fudge ice cream topping.
- Chop the turtle candies and cover the top of the salted caramel and fudge.
- Add a layer of salted pecans and repeat the layers.

I placed the homemade whipped cream in a pastry bag with a 1C pastry tip and made swirls around the edges of the pudding. I added Nilla Wafers, sliced banana, and turtle candies to the swirls. I finished the pudding off with additional salted pecans in the center.

Not only was I finished in the hour allotted, but it looked beautiful. Family and neighbors had bragged about the tastes many times. I knew it was going to be a hit.

Before the first judge was ready for his sample, I had dipped out a perfect sample cup with a little bit of everything on it.

While waiting on the judges to announce the winners, Floy took Caleb for a walk around the craft vendors. One of the vendors approached them. He recognized Caleb had special needs. He said he had something special for him. Floy and Caleb followed him back to his craft table, where he handed him a jumbo Clifford Big Red Dog stuffed animal.

At the time, Clifford was one of Caleb's favorite public television shows. Caleb held him tightly for the rest of the day. He was so proud of his Clifford. It was worth the trip to see his massive grin the rest of the day.

The time came for them to announce the winners. I hoped to make it into the top three. I was a little sad to hear my name called in the four through ten spots. My disappointment didn't last long. Only ten people were selected to participate each year. Just being a part of the competition made me a winner.

I was genuinely thankful for having the opportunity to compete in the National Banana Pudding Contest. I know only God could have opened this door.

CHAPTER TWELVE

HARDSHIPS WILL COME

Grow through what you go through.

As soon as Caleb could sit up by himself, I would place him on the kitchen counter to help me cook, especially bake. His therapist said to do things with repetition to help his memory and processing. I used baking to help him, which we both loved. We baked the same two things, chocolate chip cookies and pound cakes.

Over the years, Caleb learned not only the ingredients, but the amounts in each recipe and how to make them. We shared the baked goods with everyone we could think of, including our neighbors Glenn and Fran, the students at Carly's school, firemen at the local fire department, and our friends from church. Most of all, Caleb loved sharing pound cake with Glenn and Fran. Each time, they would go on and on about how they couldn't believe he made the best pound cake ever.

He would beam with pride. Stand a little taller. It warmed my heart to see Caleb happy. It made me want to get in the kitchen with Caleb again as soon as possible. Here is Caleb's pound cake recipe:

- 1 cup butter, softened
- $\frac{1}{2}$ cup butter flavored shortening

- 3 cups of sugar
- 5 eggs
- $\frac{3}{4}$ cup sour cream
- 1 tablespoon butter flavoring
- 2 tablespoons pure vanilla extract
- 3 cups all-purpose flour
- 1 teaspoon salt
- 1 teaspoon baking powder
- $\frac{3}{4}$ cup buttermilk

1. Preheat the oven 325 degrees.
2. With an electric mixer, cream together 1 cup butter, softened, and 1/2 cup butter flavored shortening.
3. Add 3 cups of sugar to the creamed butter and shortening. This is an important step. Cream these ingredients for 3 to 5 minutes until it is nice and fluffy.
4. Mix in five eggs one at a time just until each one disappears. About 1 to 2 minutes.
5. Blend in 3/4 cup of sour cream.
6. Add 1 tablespoon butter flavoring and 2 tablespoons pure vanilla extract.
7. Sift the flour, baking powder, and salt together.
8. Alternate the flour mixture with 3/4 cup buttermilk just until blended.
9. Grease and flour a 12-cup Bundt pan.
10. Bake 325 degrees for 1 hour and 15 minutes. Allow the cake to

cool completely for about 20 to 30 minutes. Insert a toothpick in the center. It should not have wet cake on it.

You may have noticed that this book is a lot about hardships with recipes thrown in periodically. That's sort of been the story of my life. It's been filled with an incredible number of difficult situations. Baking has always been interwoven through the fabric of my life. Through the good times and the bad.

Always bringing me joy in the midst of the suffering. My kitchen was like an oasis. An escape. The place I could go to retain my sanity. When I'm baking, I don't think about the problems. They're still there when I finish, but for a little while, I'm lost in my own world. It's like they don't exist for those few hours when I'm cooking.

Robert Schuller once said that tough times never last, but tough people do. My experience has been that sometimes, tough times do last. They keep going and going. Like they have a life of their own. Trouble is sometimes like a treadmill you can never get off of.

Caleb's problems will last his entire life. That doesn't mean we haven't learned to cope with them. It doesn't mean he's not one of the greatest joys in my life. It's just that tough people can't necessarily overcome the problems through sheer determination.

Sometimes you just have to buckle your seatbelt and endure it. Look for the joy where you can find it. Life isn't always fair. We don't all get the same proportionate amount of trouble.

For my family, as soon as we solved one problem, another one surfaced. You've heard the saying, "when it rains it pours." For us, when it poured, it kept on raining. Only harder. It never stopped. When it seemed like the rain was letting up, it was only the calm before the storm. A monsoon would hit. Then it flooded. If the flood didn't destroy everything, then the tornado did.

I don't know why it's been that way for us. I've asked the Lord. We faced a lot of hardships over an extended period of time. I'm not complaining, just sharing my story.

For one reason.

So you can be encouraged.

How does the pain and heartache my family went through encourage you?

By showing you it's possible to get through it with God's help.

I don't know how people do it without God. I remember when I didn't have God to help me. The first part of my life was filled with unspeakable pain. Without God to help me. I felt so alone. I was a young girl trying to cope with problems beyond my ability to solve.

Although, in retrospect, even during those dark times I can see how God was with me.

After I became a Christian, the problems didn't get easier. I just was able to handle them better. I know God was with me through Jerry's alcoholism and Caleb's medical issues.

As I got older, the problems intensified. Some were my own fault. Others were caused by accidents. Some were because of the hand dealt to me. The trouble was always difficult regardless of the source.

Why do I share some of those in this book? This memoir is not my catharsis. It's not my attempt to get it all out and on paper so that I might feel better. This is also not a "woe is me" book. I'm not seeking pity or for anyone to feel sorry for me.

I wrote this memoir for you. In all honesty, I didn't really want to relive the pain. I did it because God told me to.

Above all else, this book is a book about overcoming. About faith. About facing life's challenges head on and never giving up. Not giving up on your marriage. Not giving up on your children. Not giving up on God. Not giving up on your calling to compete in cooking contests just because you don't always win.

As I began to grow in my faith, it became tested again and again through troubles and hardships. Up to this point, I've chronicled many of the challenges I faced.

Little did I know, the worst was still to come.

* * *

When my twin boys were fifteen months old, I loaded them up and headed to pick Carly up from school, as we did every day. Carly was telling me about her day. I glanced back at the boys. At the same time, the car in front of me made a quick stop. When I looked up, I had no time to stop. I hit the car in front of me, who hit a car, who hit a car, who hit another car. It was a chain reaction, and I started the whole thing.

I looked around to see if Carly, Casey, and Caleb were okay. They were.

My heart did several somersaults when I saw the damage to the cars in front of me.

What have I done?

I quickly got out of the car to see if the other people were okay. Thank God, everyone was fine. We all walked away from the wreck. No one needed an ambulance at the time. Later that evening, I found out the lady I hit went to the emergency room. She wasn't wearing her seatbelt, and her knees hit the dash.

As it happened, this woman often sat in front of my family at church. We greeted each other every Sunday. Even before the accident, she had knee problems and rarely stood, but her special needs daughter would always stand and greet us.

A couple of months later, we got a letter in the mail. Jerry opened it. I knew something was wrong when he started furrowing his eyebrows, and he rested his chin between his thumb and index finger while leaning on the counter.

"What is it?" I asked.

"Margaret from church is suing us for $275,000. That's more than the limit on our insurance policy."

I could hardly believe the words coming out of his mouth. She wasn't really hurt that badly. Certainly not bad enough to demand that kind of money.

Who sues someone they go to church with?

I started sobbing uncontrollably. Remembering it was all my fault.

What were we going to do? We didn't have that kind of money. At that time, we hadn't finished paying off the debt from Caleb's hospital stay.

"I'm so sorry," I said to Jerry, as tears flowed from my face.

Jerry reassured me God was in control and was going to take care of it. He continued telling me everything was going to be okay. Unfortunately, I had my doubts. I felt like I deserved this mess for not paying attention.

I'd had several nightmares about the accident. Now those nightmares were becoming real in ways I never thought possible. A legal battle can become all consuming. For months, it was all I could think about. I had such a hard time getting to sleep. Every time I closed my eyes, I could hear the crash.

Finally, I turned it over to God. There wasn't anything I could do about it anyway. When I did, a peace came over me and it no longer interrupted my sleep. The problem didn't go away, but my fear did.

A few months later, I received a phone call from my insurance company saying they couldn't settle the issue out of court and that

I'd be getting a letter with a court date. I wanted desperately for it to go away, but I spent every day on my knees, asking God to take the burden from me.

Glenn, our neighbor, also went to church with us and one day asked me for an update on my lawsuit. I shared with him the status. That the woman was still suing us and wouldn't settle.

The next day, unbeknownst to me, Glenn spoke with our preacher. Within a week, the insurance company informed me they had settled. The woman had accepted an amount from my insurance company for her car, medical expenses, and suffering.

The insurance company paid my debt in full.

A tremendous burden was gone. Once again, God used Glenn to help me.

Sometimes the problems are our own fault. I didn't cause the accident on purpose, but I could've been more careful. That didn't mean I couldn't turn to God to help me through it.

* * *

April 1999

One evening, as I sat and held Caleb before bed, the left side of his body began twitching. I held him tight as his body continued to twitch. Caleb was now two years and eight months old. He'd been off seizure medicine since he was four months old.

We took him to the emergency room, and they admitted him for observation and an EEG. Unfortunately, it was seizures, and Caleb needed to go back on medicine. After our phenobarbital experience, I was concerned that the medicine would alter his personality, and I would no longer get to hear the contagious belly laughter he was famous for.

The good news was that his new medicine worked. Caleb's seizures were brought under control, and his belly was back shaking like a bowl full of jelly.

Caleb still suffered from migraines though. Numerous CT scans proved the migraines weren't shunt related.

After a year on phenobarbital, we were able to slowly transition Caleb to a new drug called Topamax. Instead of having two or three headaches a week, he had one or two a month. Overall, Caleb was doing much better.

A few months later, a new problem arose. Caleb had to have his tonsils removed. A normal procedure for most kids. Not for someone with Caleb's condition.

We chose to have the surgery in Montgomery, Alabama, where we lived, instead of going to the Children's hospital in Atlanta, where Caleb had all his brain surgeries.

An immediate problem was getting an IV into Caleb's veins which were shot from all the procedures he'd had over the years. I tried hard to explain to the anesthesiologist Caleb's veins were shot. He had probably heard that many times and he reassured me he would find one.

After Caleb's tonsil surgery, they wheeled him into the recovery room where I was sitting. To my horror, the first thing I saw was a large needle stuck out of the side of Caleb's neck. The worst possible spot after having tonsils removed. Obviously, the anesthesiologist hadn't been able to get an IV in his arm.

Momma bear was ready to explode.

When I attempted to stand, the chair I was sitting in was on wheels and came out from under me. I hit my forehead on the floor. The next thing I knew, doctors and nurses hovered over me. I tried to tell them I was okay, but they seemed to think differently.

As they put me on the stretcher, I noticed the puddle of blood on the floor. When I asked what happened, a nurse told me I passed out and had hit my head. I needed stitches. As they rolled me away, I begged them to get Jerry to stay with Caleb. All I could think about was Caleb recovering without me. He couldn't communicate how he was feeling.

I was also concerned about Jerry having a son in the recovery room and a wife in the emergency room. I knew he couldn't be in two places at once. I wanted to make sure Jerry knew to stay with Caleb.

I ended up with twenty-two stitches in the middle of my forehead.

God was with me in every way. He even provided a plastic surgeon who happened to be in the emergency room to stitch up my head.

I would love to tell you we never went back to that hospital, but they saved Caleb's life six months later.

* * *

July 3rd

Six months later, we had to rush Caleb back to the same hospital in Montgomery. The strangest thing had happened. Caleb was in the backyard playing. He ran to retrieve a ball that had rolled under a shrub.

When he came back to where I was standing, he was as white as a sheet. Like he was in shock. Fear was all over his face. I knew immediately that something was wrong. My heart pounded in my ears as I tried to figure out what it was.

I began asking Caleb yes and no questions. He rarely spoke given his processing problems and all the many surgeries he'd endured. He was also afraid of doctors and hospitals, so he was hesitant to tell me if something was wrong.

For whatever reason, I asked Caleb if he'd been bitten by a snake. He nodded.

The thought had just popped into my mind. I think it came from the Holy Spirit telling me what was wrong with my child.

It's a good thing I figured it out.

I began to search his hands and arms. I raised his right arm and looked it over. Next, I raised his left arm and searched. I figured it would be on his hands or arms since he reached for the ball in the shrubs.

I found it!

Three bite marks were on his left hand, pointer finger.

I looked Caleb in his eyes and asked him,

"Did a snake bite you?" His eyes got huge as if he was trying to tell me yes by using his eyes.

I picked him up and raced to the car and to the pediatrician's office, which was closer than the hospital. I went straight to the counter and said I had a child with a possible snake bite. Luckily, a doctor was standing there. She opened the door to the office and let us in. The next thing I knew, we were surrounded by pediatricians. All the doctors in the office came running to see Caleb.

Caleb's hand was extremely swollen. The doctors confirmed that it looked like a poisonous snake bite. One of them told me she would call the emergency room and for me to drive him straight there. She said Caleb needed a generic antivenom since we don't know what kind of snake bit him.

As we left, the doctor assured us they'd pray. I ran to the car with Caleb in my arms and headed to the hospital.

This was the hospital that had messed up Caleb's IV during his tonsil surgery. When I left the hospital with Caleb that day, I vowed to never return there.

I considered my options. That hospital was the closest one.

So I sped out of the parking lot to get there as soon as possible.

My heart was pounding so fast, I could hear it in my ears.

From the tone in the doctor's voice, I knew Caleb's situation was life threatening.

All the way to the hospital, I prayed and asked God for a miracle and to do what only He could do. By the time we reached the emergency room, I had an unexplainable peace that everything was going to be okay.

Later I found out the hospital had the only generic antivenom in the entire state!

They had six bags. After finding a place for his IV in his leg, he was given five bags of antivenom over the next three days. Because it was July 3rd and a busy time of the year for snake bites, they saved a bag for another emergency.

God had answered my prayers. If I had taken Caleb to a different hospital, he might not have survived the snake bite.

God was with us every step of that terrifying event. The hospital ended up saving my son's life. The one I vowed I'd never go back to. I have learned to never say never to God.

He has a way of taking my worst fear and turning it into something good.

CHAPTER THIRTEEN

ENDLESS EMERGENCY BRAIN SURGERIES

Struggle is part of the journey.

Christmas

By this time, Jerry's job situation had stabilized, and he was able to be home more. He accepted a new job in medical capital sales with a smaller territory which meant less travel. Jerry wanted to be home to help with the kids and I needed the help.

Having a special needs child who required around the clock care was hard enough. To have a child go from one near death experience to another over and over again was beyond excruciating. It took me to the limit of my faith on more than one occasion.

I hope I haven't given you the wrong impression. That I'm some model of faith for you to emulate. That I'm trying to paint a picture of a strong pillar of spiritual fortitude who belongs in the Hall of Faith in Hebrews 11.

Quite the contrary.

Through these dark times, I had many moments of doubt and un-belief. Sometimes, the fear was so strong I thought I wasn't going to be able to stand it.

And yes, there were even times when I was mad at God.

None more so than Christmas of 2003.

* * *

Our family went to Gainesboro Tennessee to visit Grammy and Gramps, Don and Floy. When we arrived, they were already on the porch waiting for us. Caleb was the first one out of the car and ran as fast as he could to greet them. He wobbled from side to side due to his cerebral palsy on his left side but was determined to get there first.

The boy amazed me. He'd had emergency brain surgery a couple of weeks before for a shunt failure and there he was grinning from ear to ear, bounding around with energy, while the rest of us were dragging, exhausted from the trip.

The surgery had made Caleb's headaches instantly better, which was part of the reason Caleb was feeling as good as he was, and a reason why we even considered making the trip. That whole evening was a wonderful time for Caleb and all of us as we anticipated a Christmas together free from health problems and anxiety.

Things were looking up and I was optimistic that this would be the best Christmas ever.

The next morning, Caleb got out of bed and immediately buried his face into my side. My heart sank to the bottom of my chest. I knew my son well enough to know what that meant.

He had a severe headache. Which meant his shunt was failing.

I wanted to scream at the top of my lungs.

I immediately got Jerry.

"What should we do?" he asked.

"Let's take him to the emergency room in Cookeville," I said. "It's closer than Atlanta. They can do a CT scan to see if it's a shunt failure."

We rushed Caleb over there. The doctors at the emergency room didn't have Caleb's latest scans to compare to the one they did. Caleb's slit ventricles made it difficult for them to tell if his shunt was failing.

We had two options. Go drive an hour and a half to Vanderbilt or drive four and half hours to Atlanta. Dr. Henry in Atlanta would know what to do so that's what we decided. As much as I hated to leave our family holiday, we set out on the long drive and prayed the whole way that Caleb wouldn't die in my arms.

We called ahead and Dr. Henry was at the emergency room of Children's Hospital in Atlanta to meet us.

We started using Dr. Henry in Atlanta after moving from Tennessee to Atlanta, Georgia. Dr. Henry came highly recommended by Caleb's pediatric neurosurgeon in Nashville. Even though we had moved from Atlanta to Montgomery, Alabama, we decided to keep going to Dr. Henry for all of Caleb's surgeries.

Jerry and I trusted him. We understood the risks and complications of shunt failures and brain surgeries. We never blamed Dr. Henry for Caleb's shunt failures, external drain issues, or infections. We knew he was doing everything he could to help Caleb.

On our way to Atlanta, we called Grammy and Gramps to tell them we were driving Caleb to Children's Hospital in Atlanta. We asked them to pray for us and thanked them for watching the kids. Everyone, including the kids, knew if Caleb's shunt failed, he needed emergency surgery. They had been through this routine many times.

On the way, Caleb's condition worsened. So did my mood. I was sinking into a depression. We were all so excited about Christmas together. Carly and Casey would be devastated if we didn't make it back in time to open presents with them. It was several days before Christmas and, on the phone, I had assured them we'd be back in time, although I couldn't know for sure.

What if we couldn't? I felt like such a failure as a mom. Caleb got so much of our attention. Christmas was so important to me. I didn't have a mother around at Christmas. I never wanted that for my kids.

Even worse, what would future Christmases be like if Caleb died this Christmas?

I had to get those negative thoughts out of my mind. A lot of thoughts can come into your head on such a long drive. It felt like every fear in the world was bombarding me at once.

By the time we arrived at the hospital emergency room, Caleb's blood pressure was high, and his pulse was low. He was in bad shape. Caleb was put on a stretcher and taken immediately into surgery. They didn't even bother doing another CT scan. It was obvious to Dr. Henry what was wrong with Caleb.

While Caleb was in surgery, Jerry and I prayed. As we always did in these situations. We thanked God that we had made it to Children's in Atlanta and trusted Him for a good outcome.

Jerry was such an encouragement to me. "Focus on all the times God has been with Caleb and answered our prayers," he said.

I smiled and agreed with him, but he didn't know the inner turmoil I was feeling.

This time felt different.

I wasn't sure we had made the right decision driving to Atlanta. Shunt failures are a matter of life or death. Since Caleb can't communicate, it's hard to know what to do. I worried our decision to go to Atlanta might have caused him extra brain damage, not to mention could've killed him.

"We should've taken him to Vanderbilt in Nashville," I finally said to Jerry, when I couldn't hold it in any longer.

Vanderbilt was only an hour and a half from Cookeville. When Caleb was a baby, a pediatric neurosurgeon performed several surgeries on Caleb.

"It doesn't do any good to second guess it now," Jerry said. "We'll just have to hope for the best."

The next few hours were excruciating as all we could do was wait.

When I finally saw Dr. Henry walking toward us with a big smile on his face, I knew the surgery had gone well.

"Caleb is going to be okay," Dr. Henry said. "He's in recovery and will be moved to a room shortly."

"Thank God! We've been praying for you and Caleb," I said.

I felt bad that I'd ever doubted God to begin with.

When Caleb was brought back to recovery, he wasn't speaking to me. I could see the anger on his face.

Although Caleb was seven years old, he rarely communicated. Because he'd been in and out of hospitals so much and experienced so much pain and trauma, he was growing mistrustful of even me. I tried to reassure him, but the words sounded hollow. Even to me.

I'd told him these things before. Assured him that everything was going to be okay. That God was looking out for him.

How could I expect Caleb to believe me when I was having my own doubts now?

Every time it looked like Caleb was doing better, something bad would happen and we'd be back in the hospital.

How many prayers did I have to pray before this stopped happening to us?

Caleb would get better and my faith would soar. Then something like this would happen. As hard as it was on us, it was harder on Caleb by an incalculable amount. While I felt fear, he felt it even more, times ten.

I was frustrated. Caleb had to be wondering if it was ever going to end.

Not only was he traumatized, but his selective mutism and processing problems made it extremely difficult for him to communicate how he was feeling. Even when he wasn't in pain and feeling well, he was beginning to be much quieter, even with me.

I don't think Caleb trusted me anymore. He feared us taking him back to the hospital. He certainly didn't understand why he had to be in such pain and have surgery after surgery. Especially when I kept telling him everything was going to be okay.

Within an hour he was moved to a room, but it wasn't long before he began having a severe headache. He rooted his head into his pillow to try to find comfort.

My heart broke.

Caleb wouldn't look at me nor answer any of my questions. I knew his shunt was failing again, but he'd just had surgery a few hours ago.

I called for the nurses. They weren't convinced it was shunt failure. We were told to try and make it through the night and Dr. Henry would see him in the morning.

Caleb was in so much pain, I could barely stand it.

I wanted to scream.

With God's help, we made it through the night. Somehow.

The following morning, a CT confirmed another shunt failure. Caleb had another emergency surgery.

I was angry.

How much could one child take?

Is this what his life was going to be like?

Going from one crisis to another. One shunt failure to another. Headaches, day after day. Always wondering if the next headache would be the one that killed him.

After receiving a new shunt, Caleb seemed to be doing much better, and we were able to go home to Montgomery, Christmas Eve morning.

The trip from Atlanta to Montgomery seemed to take forever. By the time we arrived, we were all worn out but couldn't wait to see everyone. Grammy and Gramps had driven Carly and Casey back to Montgomery from Tennessee, and we were all looking forward to being together for Christmas.

Even though we were exhausted, we gave each other endless hugs and thanked God for allowing us to be together. It could be worse. We could still be back in Atlanta.

By Christmas Eve, Caleb was once again rooting his face in a pillow to find comfort. As I turned his head around to see his face, I knew his shunt had failed again. I could see the pain in his face and eyes. I was physically, spiritually, and emotionally drained, and I could not imagine the disappointment and pain he was feeling.

We had to drive back to Atlanta.

My jaw clenched. My fists were in a ball. I wanted to throw something. I was so angry.

It's Christmas. Can't we have one day of peace?

I cried out to God. I blamed Him. How many prayers had we prayed?

All the way to Atlanta, I asked God why He would punish an innocent child. God had the power to fix all these shunt problems, but He hadn't. I began to wonder if God really loved me. If He didn't love me, He loved Caleb. Shouldn't He want to heal Caleb in spite of me?

I felt guilty. Like it was my fault Caleb wasn't healed. What did I do to deserve this?

I begged God to take this heartache from me.

I didn't feel any better. Those prayers certainly weren't helping. Regardless of how I felt, Caleb was on death's door again. My doubts and emotions weren't doing him any good at that moment. All I could do was wipe away the tears and try to muster up enough strength and faith to get through another surgery.

We called ahead so the emergency room would know we were coming and to call Dr. Henry.

The last thing the woman on the phone said before hanging up was, "I'm so sorry."

Yeah. So am I. I thought to myself angrily. So am I.

* * *

Surgery #3

On Christmas morning, Caleb was doing a lot better. Dr. Henry was going to release him to go home in the afternoon if he was still doing better. We called Carly and Casey to tell them the good news. We also told them to go ahead and open their Christmas presents. After all, they were children, and I didn't want to make their Christmas worse by not letting them open their gifts.

We listened on the phone as Carly and Casey opened their gifts. I was so thankful for Caleb doing better, but it broke my heart to miss Christmas morning with my other kids. My heart felt like it was ripping out of my chest. I had flashbacks of every Christmas morning as a teen when my mother wasn't there.

I could tell this was taking a toll on my other kids as well.

As I listened to them open their presents, I felt angry at God for not allowing us to be together and begged Him to allow us to go home soon. Later that afternoon, Dr. Henry came by to check on Caleb.

He said we could go home. I was elated and, for a moment, my resentment toward God was tamped down. I said a quick prayer thanking Him for letting Caleb go home.

Everything was already packed in anticipation. If the doctor hadn't said we could go home, I don't know what I would've done. I was close to spiraling out of control, emotionally, physically, and spiritually. Like I was on the brink of my own breakdown.

We made the long drive home and arrived around dinnertime. Jerry, Caleb, and I were starving. We managed to scramble some eggs and fry some bacon for our Christmas dinner.

The anger returned with a vengeance.

I always cooked Christmas dinner. Made a big spread for everyone. Cooking was my passion. Christmas dinner always brought me great joy watching everyone eat the feast I made for them.

That moment was being robbed from me. We were having eggs and bacon! With no dessert!

My father-in-law must've sensed my disappointment. He said, "It's okay. What we eat doesn't matter. What matters is our family enjoying a meal together and thanking God for all He has done. We will have many more Christmas dinners with all the trimmings."

That changed my attitude. I was grateful to be home on Christmas. I thanked God for guiding us safely home and giving Caleb a working shunt and apologized to God for having so much anger and for doubting Him.

The rest of the evening was fun for everyone. We were all mindful of the fact that Caleb was alive. He could've easily not survived the ordeal. That was something to be thankful for and I reminded everyone of that fact several times.

In the back of my mind, though, I couldn't help but wonder if something was going to happen to ruin things.

* * *

Surgery #4

Over the next week, Caleb began to have a lot of pain in his stomach. We took him to see his local pediatrician, and she treated him for constipation. But using the bathroom didn't help. Something was wrong. On New Year's Eve, we rushed Caleb back to Atlanta to see his neurosurgeon.

Dr. Henry did a spinal tap. The results weren't good. I could see it on Dr. Henry's face.

"Caleb has a shunt infection—pseudomonas," Dr. Henry said. "Caleb needs his shunt removed and an external drain put in, which will drain his spinal fluid on the outside of his body. The external drain will remain until his infection is clear—about ten days."

He scheduled surgery for the following morning.

I got quiet as the news sunk in. Dr. Henry asked if we had any questions.

"Pseudomonas was a risk of surgery and he got it," I said. "I went through this nightmare before when Caleb had staph in his brain as a baby. It was weeks before the infection cleared up."

"Yes," Dr. Henry said. "That's the risk of having so many surgeries."

Ventriculoperitoneal shunt placement is common for hydrocephalus but can have many complications, including shunt infections, especially in children. The risk of infection is even higher for external drains. Shunt infections can show up weeks after surgery. The more shunt surgeries the higher risk and rate of infection. The risk of shunt infections would always be high for Caleb until he kept a shunt working.

Dr. Henry continued, "The infection control doctor, bug doctor, will visit with Caleb to explain the treatment plan."

After finding out this news, I sent Jerry home to Montgomery. Caleb was going to be there for a while.

I stood outside Caleb's door and waved goodbye to Jerry until I could no longer see him. Once he was gone, I felt so alone. Tears streamed down my face. My feet were frozen to the floor. Like I was paralyzed and couldn't move.

What was I going to do? Did I have the strength for another long stint in the hospital? How was Caleb going to survive it?

What made it even worse was that I had to go through those doors into Caleb's room and face my child. Explain to him what was happening.

I tried.

"You have a bug in your stomach and need ten days of medicine to get rid of it," I said. My voice cracked. "Let's count the days down until you can get a new shunt and go home."

I could see in his eyes that he didn't believe me.

"Momma's not going anywhere," I said. "I'll be by your side every minute of every day. We'll go through this together."

He smiled painfully.

He was in the hospital for weeks, not days. I worked hard trying to explain the medical procedures to him without worrying him unnecessarily. I would distract him by watching Disney movies with him, playing cards, board games, coloring, spoiling him with toys, reading books, and even candy.

I did everything I could to help him get better, but there was little I could do. Caleb was fighting a battle of shunt failures, infections, extreme headaches, and more brain damage. I could not make his brain accept a foreign object in it and certainly couldn't make it drain spinal fluid correctly like it was supposed to do.

I couldn't make his body fight the infection. Couldn't make the antibiotics work.

I felt hopeless.

My first instinct was to lash out at God again. But what good would that do?

I needed God's help. The Bible says He is hope for the hopeless. He is peace when we need peace. He's your help in times of trouble.

Without faith, it's impossible to please Him. He responds to our faith.

So many times in the past, I'd prayed and God had helped us. Maybe Caleb wasn't completely healed, but that didn't mean God didn't love me or that He didn't love Caleb. We have an enemy in this world. I can't explain all the reasons why Caleb had to suffer.

But what I did know was that being angry at God wasn't going to help Caleb or me.

I couldn't make the medical procedures work, but I could pray. I could be there for Caleb. Let him see my faith. In reality, other than providing him with motherly care, that's all I could really do for him.

If I was failing Caleb, it was in doubting God.

I needed to show Caleb that I trusted God. I needed my son to see me praying. Asking God for mercy. For strength and comfort. For healing. For wisdom to make good decisions regarding Caleb's care.

That attitude made all the difference. We still had to endure the suffering, but I could tell God was with us.

It helped Caleb as well. I'm convinced it's how he found the strength to fight. The will to live. Eventually, we were able to go home.

It taught me a great lesson. Praying for my family and trusting God, remembering how he had helped us in the past, and standing on the promises through prayer was the most powerful thing I could do for my son and my family.

"Cast thy burden upon the Lord, and he shall sustain thee: he shall never suffer the righteous to be moved." (Psalm 55:22 KJV)

When our church family in Montgomery found out about Caleb being in the hospital, they called to encourage us. We even had a surprise visit from several friends from church. They came with a carload of gifts, including snacks, magazines, coloring books, candy, toys, and even change for the drink machine.

That was such a blessing.

When I was feeling unloved, they overwhelmed me with God's love. I learned through pain I needed others to help carry my burdens.

Landmark Church will always be near and dear to our hearts.

"Beloved, let us love one another; because love is of God, and every one that loves has been begotten of God, and knows God." (1 John 4:7 DARBY)

CHAPTER FOURTEEN
GOD SENT AN ANGEL

Finding hope in the struggle.

We needed some good news. Caleb had just endured the worst stretch of his young life. Numerous surgeries. Shunt failures. Headaches. Several long trips to Atlanta. Weeks away from home and my other kids.

Now Caleb had an infection and required ten days of antibiotics.

The infection control doctor, or "bug doctor," as he referred to himself, stopped by and explained, "Caleb needs three different antibiotics for ten days. After ten days, his spinal fluid will be tested to see if the infection is gone."

The ten days dragged on, but the day of testing finally arrived. *Thank God!*

Caleb was clear of the infection and the doctors scheduled to have the external drain removed and his shunt put back in. A couple days after the surgery, Jerry, Carly, and Casey arrived to take us home.

This was the break I'd been praying for. The infection was gone. Caleb had a shunt, and we could go home.

Things were looking up. So were my spirits which were soaring.

Caleb lit up when his siblings walked into the room. He'd been lying in bed for most of the ten days. He didn't fully understand why he was there and didn't like being hooked up to all the machines. He got little rest from the alarms which went off constantly and the nurses taking his vital signs continuously.

Carly and Casey jumped on the bed beside Caleb and started teasing him, as only siblings can do. They made up silly songs and even talked "toilet talk." They were trying to get him to talk. He wouldn't but they did get him to shake the whole bed with his chuckles, which was just as good. It made me a happy momma to not only hear Caleb laugh, but to see the three of them together.

We checked out of the hospital and drove home.

The joy we felt at that moment was short-lived.

We were barely back home when Caleb came down with another headache.

Without hesitation, we rushed back to Children's hospital in Atlanta. Dr. Henry removed fluid out of Caleb's shunt and had it tested.

"I'm going to admit Caleb for observation until I figure out what is going on with his shunt," Dr. Henry said.

They ran several tests. When Dr. Henry entered our room the following morning, I knew something was wrong.

"Caleb has pseudomonas again," he said. "This time it's in his head."

I could hardly believe the words coming out of his mouth.

How could that be? Caleb just finished ten days of antibiotics to get rid of pseudomonas. How could it be back this fast?

As Dr. Henry continued to speak, I lost all control of my emotions and tears.

"The infectious disease doctor will be back to see you," Dr. Henry said. "Surgery is scheduled to remove his shunt and put in an external drain on Wednesday."

Another surgery!

I couldn't even respond due to the uncontrollable sobs.

Dr. Henry walked out of the room. I caught a glimpse of his arm through the window. He had stopped and leaned back on the wall between the window and the door to Caleb's room. He put his hand on his forehead clearly in pain.

I realized at that moment how hard it must be for him as well. He really did care about Caleb. It was tearing him up inside having to take this poor child to the operating room over and over again. Each time thinking that would be the last time only to have to do it again a few days later.

At that moment, my heart broke for Dr. Henry as well. This was hard on all of us. I never blamed him, but I wondered if he blamed himself. Questioned his own abilities. What were his nights like? Were they sleepless? Did he wonder if he was ever going to be able to help Caleb.

It seemed like Dr. Henry was doing everything he could for Caleb. Every time a surgery was scheduled, he really had no other choice. Caleb would die without the surgeries.

He might die in surgery which was part of what made it so excruciating.

Our lives for several months had been continual trauma. Going from one life or death situation to another.

Dr. Henry had to be feeling a similar stress. He was the one performing the surgeries. He always seemed to agree with me when I told him I was praying for him and for Caleb and that God was using him to help my son through this ordeal.

What if his faith was wavering as well?

I couldn't have that. I needed the doctor to be strong. Confident in his abilities. Caleb needed him to be at the top of his game. After seeing Dr. Henry upset, I wish I hadn't broken down in front of him.

The doctor needed to see my faith. I wanted him to know God was in charge. That it wasn't his fault. I also wanted him to know my God was a big God who had helped me so many times in the past. I had no doubt God was going to get my family through this heartache as well.

I prayed and gave Caleb's situation to God. I asked God to give me the strength to make it through the next ten days and to help me be a shining light of hope to everyone around me, including Dr. Henry.

While Caleb napped, I walked down the hall and noticed the other patients. I felt God whisper, *count your blessings*. Several of them were dealing with worse problems, including head trauma and cancer. I prayed for them each time I passed their rooms. I knew those kids were fighting for their lives and their mothers were dealing with overwhelming heartache as well.

I wondered if they were dealing with the enormous pain without God. I couldn't imagine.

It helped me put my situation in perspective. Most of the kids on that floor were fighting for their lives as well.

Caleb may not have been as bad as some, but his situation couldn't have been much worse. He needed three weeks of strong IV antibiotics before he could get a new shunt. He'd have to be sedated and a PICC line put in because the antibiotics were too strong for his veins.

We were back to square one. Every time we thought our lives were going to get back to some sense of normalcy, Caleb had a complication and had to start the long process of drugs and surgeries all over again.

My faith was as weak as Caleb's health. The strength I had tapped into that helped me get through the last few weeks of torture was gone. I didn't know if I had the ability to regain it and endure this all over again. Especially since this time, the doctors made it sound like it'd be worse than before. If that were even possible.

I did the only thing I knew to do. Talk to God. Share with Him the good and the bad. Not pretend to be okay. Not to pretend to be a strong woman of faith. But come to Him in my weakness.

This was basically the prayer I prayed to God in my head.

God, I have tried to be positive during all the pain Caleb has had to suffer, but I don't know how much more I can endure. I don't know how much more he can endure. How do I explain this to him? More surgeries. More weeks in the hospital. He'll blame me. Please help me! I'm hundreds of miles away from home and the support of my family. I can't stand it. I can't handle this much sorrow. I need you, Lord!

I'd like to say I had a huge spiritual awakening, and my spirits were immediately lifted. All I can say was I did what I could. Honestly, we can all endure a lot more than we think we can when push comes to shove.

I felt like someone was trying to shove me off a cliff and I was resisting it with all my strength.

What choice did I have?

The only other option was Caleb dying. Giving up. That wasn't an acceptable option. I knew my son was going to live. That God had a plan for his life. We'd see it when we got to the other side of the trial.

Whatever I had to endure, would be much worse for Caleb. So, I had to be strong for him.

I spent every day reading God's Word out loud so I could hear God's voice and so Caleb could hear me.

I had my moments. I'm not going to lie. I asked God some difficult questions. Where are you? Why me? Why does Caleb have to be in so much pain all the time? Why do we have to be separated from our family? How do I find the words to comfort my son? How can I convey to the doctor that everything's going to be okay?

Will it really be okay, God?

God felt so far away. But I kept reading His Word, praying, asking questions, and begging for His help.

I thought back to the time when I had a gun pointed at my head as a teenager and I prayed to God for the first time to help me and He did. I drew strength from that memory.

Even if it didn't seem like it at times, God was helping us. I'd prayed for Caleb many times. He was still alive. Barely hanging on, but we still had hope.

God could handle my questions. He wasn't mad at me for asking them.

I'd like to say that Caleb's condition improved when I prayed. It didn't. Caleb's condition didn't improve with the antibiotics.

He was in so much pain. That made it so much harder.

My heart broke for my little boy.

He'd turn sideways in the hospital bed and root his head in his pillow. He normally slept on his back but now he put his forehead down first in pain. He didn't have a shunt so I was confused as to what could be causing the headaches. It could only mean that fluid wasn't draining from his head. That his external drain was failing.

I pleaded with the nurses to do something. After the nurses talked to the neurosurgeon, Caleb was started on Demerol every two hours for his pain. He slept a lot, but when he was awake, he was in pain and would root his head into his pillow. Even with the powerful pain reliever, strong enough to knock out a horse.

In reality, all Demerol could do was mask the pain. It wasn't resolving the issue. Caleb would always have pain until the swelling in his brain was resolved.

Dr. Henry wasn't on call that first weekend. So, we saw one of his partners. When the doctor arrived, I told him Caleb had been in extreme pain for days. He explained the drain was working but not draining as much fluid as it had been, which caused the headaches. An operation was needed to replace the drain.

Another operation!

Even though I feared the risks of another shunt surgery, including a brain bleed and infection, I knew surgery was the only way Caleb was going to get relief from fluid causing pressure in his brain.

When the doctor got into surgery, he decided to add a second external drain and leave the first one in place. Now, Caleb had two external drains. The risk of infection was high with one. What was the risk with two?

The new drain did seem to work, and Caleb began to feel better. I was relieved but knew my son wasn't out of the woods yet.

Caleb grew quieter and quieter with each surgery, and his surgeries weren't over. He looked to me to help him each time he was in pain. He didn't understand that I couldn't help, and it ripped my heart out.

At some point, he quit reaching out. By ignoring me and not making eye contact with me, I knew he was blaming me for his pain and all his surgeries. As a mom, that might've been the hardest part.

The helplessness.

I knew Caleb loved me, but I worried he didn't trust me anymore. He was tired and couldn't take much more pain or surgeries. I tried to stay positive around him, never revealing my sorrow, but instead spoiling him rotten and giving him something to look forward to.

If Caleb ever gave up hope, the end would come quickly. The only reason he was still alive was because of his strong will to live. I had to do what I could to let him know I was still fighting for him.

The doctor said Caleb needed another surgery to remove the external drains and to put the shunt back in.

I dreaded having to tell him.

* * *

You must be kidding me!

Dr. Henry came into Caleb's room and informed us that he was recommending another surgery for Caleb.

A cranial decompression.

Caleb had already endured eight surgeries in two months. This one sounded the riskiest of them all.

Dr. Henry wanted to remove part of Caleb's skull.

"The brain is encased in bone, so there's no room for swelling," Dr. Henry explained. "When the brain swells it puts tremendous pressure on it. Removing part of his skull allows room for his brain to swell. It will help with headaches and even some shunt failures."

The thoughts swirled around inside my head like an eddy.

I wanted to burst into tears but fought them back. I promised God I would set a good example for Dr. Henry.

He continued, "You'll have to be extremely careful with Caleb's head. He won't have a skull to protect parts of his brain. It will only be covered with skin."

He began to demonstrate on Caleb's head.

"I'll cut his skull open above one ear across the top of his head to the top of his other ear. A quarter-size piece of his skull will be removed above each ear on both sides of his head. He'll still be able to do normal activities but will need a helmet when active. He'll have a large scar with staples from one side to the other. His hair will grow back and cover it. This surgery is optional, so you need to make the decision."

Are you crazy? I thought. *I don't have it in me to make this decision.*

"If this was your son, would you take out part of his skull?" I asked. "This seems so extreme."

Without hesitation, Dr. Henry said, "Yes! Caleb has slit verticals. He will continue to have problems with his shunt and head swelling, which causes a lot of pain and possibly more brain damage. His ventricles are thin, which leaves little room for a shunt. If the shunt drains too much fluid or not enough fluid, it will cause headaches."

I said I'd talk to my husband and get back to him.

Jerry was home in Montgomery taking care of Carly and Casey, and trying to work. After speaking to him, we prayed about it and asked God to give us an answer.

One of my good friends, Mari Beth, called right after I got off the phone with Jerry. After explaining the decision facing us, she prayed with me. She asked God to put someone in our lives to help us make the best choice.

"God, send them an angel to show them what to do," she prayed.

That same day, Dr. Henry returned to see me. He wanted to know if one of his patients could visit us. She'd had the surgery he was recommending for Caleb. I told him that'd be great.

"What's her name?" I asked.

"Her name is Angel," he said.

* * *

Angel smiled from ear to ear when she entered Caleb's room. She clearly couldn't wait to tell me her story.

"Dr. Henry asked me to come by to visit," she said. "I had twenty shunt failures in a row before I had the cranial decompression surgery. The surgery was far better than having headaches. I haven't had any problems since my surgery."

Her mother was with her, but she didn't need her mom to help communicate her story. Angel was perfectly clear. I asked a few questions about the recovery. She explained her own experience.

I was so thankful for Angel. I told her that God had sent her to me to help me make this decision and that God had used her to encourage me.

After talking to Angel, the surgery seemed like the right thing to do. Like God was giving me the answer. If this surgery was going to help with Caleb's headaches, I was ready to make the decision. I thanked her for coming and gave her a massive hug.

After talking with Jerry, Caleb was scheduled for cranial decompression surgery. He needed to finish the round of antibiotics first and have surgery to put his shunt back.

A few days after that surgery, Caleb had cranial decompression surgery, which also went well. Afterward, Caleb's head was wrapped completely including under his chin. He looked like a mummy.

It didn't scare me because Angel had warned me, but Caleb was frustrated and scared. I was as worried about him recovering mentally from all this trauma as I was about him recovering physically.

Looking back, I can hardly believe how strong Caleb was to endure everything he did over those long and arduous weeks.

* * *

Two-and-a-half months later, Caleb was ready to go home. After ten shunt surgeries and after having part of his skull removed, the doctor said he could go home.

We were beyond excited and ready to go when Jerry arrived to pick us up. As we drove back to Montgomery, I told God I couldn't handle anything else. I was feeling sorry for myself and asking God, "Why me? Why Caleb? Is this finally over? Haven't we suffered enough?"

So many times, we'd taken Caleb home only having to rush him back to Atlanta within a few hours or days. By that point, I didn't even recognize my life. It'd been so long since I'd been home. All of my days and nights had been spent at the hospital.

I didn't think I could take it, if we had to turn around and drive back to Atlanta again.

As I held on to Caleb tightly, I remembered the words God had spoken to me in the hallway of the hospital. *Count your blessings.*

I was taking Caleb home. I was the lucky one. Some mothers at that hospital weren't able to take their child home. Some of those kids didn't make it.

Caleb was still alive. The cranial surgery had helped with the headaches. As hard as things had been, we had a lot to be thankful for.

God had sent me an Angel. If God would do that for me and for Caleb, it meant he had something special in store for us.

Tears of joy rolled down my face. I couldn't brush them away fast enough. Honestly, it'd been a long time since I felt that kind of joy. It felt good. It felt like a weight was lifting off my shoulders.

I remembered the verse in the Bible where it says to have joy when the trials come on you. Right from the beginning. Not at the end when things turned out okay.

I was learning. Growing in my faith. That was a lesson I needed to learn. To have joy even when things were hard. From the onset of the trial. The Bible says to have joy at the beginning so you can endure the trial.

I was resolved to do even better.

I knew Caleb's struggles weren't over. We'd have more things to deal with in the future. I needed to remember that moment. When joy came and overwhelmed me while we were driving home.

More importantly, I needed to learn how to tap into that joy any time I was feeling sad or depressed.

I was so happy.

God had answered my prayers and we were going home to be with family. I knew God was faithful to answer my prayers like He had done so many times in the past.

"Praise God in his sanctuary: Praise him in the firmament of his power. Praise him for his mighty acts: Praise him according to his excellent greatness. Praise him with the trumpet sound. Praise him with psaltery and harp. Praise him with timbrel and Dance. Praise him with stringed instruments and pipe. Praise him with loud cymbals: Praise him with high sounding cymbals. Let everything that hath breath praise Jehovah. Praise ye Jehovah." (Psalm 150: 1-6 ASV)

CHAPTER FIFTEEN

HIS BLADDER EXPLODED

I am fully trusting you.

I am fully trusting you.

By the title of this chapter, you may think Caleb's bladder was the one that exploded.

Thankfully, no. With everything Caleb had been through, that would've been the proverbial straw that broke the camel's back.

Someone in our family did have his bladder explode into pieces. You probably don't believe it, but it's true.

Being a traveling salesman, my husband, Jerry, was on the road constantly. He'd been in several serious automobile accidents. On three different occasions, he was hit by a log truck while on a business trip. In each incident, the truck never stopped.

It's like he was snakebit or something. Accident prone didn't even begin to describe his bad luck.

The first time a logging truck hit him, Jerry's car went into a ditch. The second time, his car spun around. The final time, the car flipped over and landed upside down in a ditch.

Fortunately, Jerry walked away from each accident without any serious injuries. But every time he left on a trip, his safety was in the back of my mind.

Whenever he walked out the door, I prayed for him until he drove away. Always having to beat the fear away. Like I was learning to do with Caleb, I had to give Jerry to God and trust that He was going to take care of him while he was traveling.

One day, the phone rang. I didn't think anything of it, until I heard a stranger's frantic voice on the other end.

"Your husband has been in a car wreck," he said.

I felt my mouth fly open. I'd been in the kitchen thinking about what to prepare for dinner. This was the last thing I expected to deal with that night.

"His car is on fire, but I drug him to safety."

On fire!

My heart started racing. It felt like it was going to jump out of my chest.

I wanted to speak, but the words didn't come. Like I was frozen in time. Unable to think, move, or act.

"He's injured and in a lot of pain," the man said.

I wondered how the man knew to call me.

As if on cue, he said, "Your husband gave me your number. The ambulance is on the way. They will take him to the hospital in Evergreen."

I hung up the phone slowly. Stunned. Trying to process everything.

If Jerry was able to give him my number, it meant he was alive. And conscious. At least enough to be able to think and speak.

I quickly gathered the kids. Carly was eleven, and Casey and Caleb were six. We sped to Evergreen, which was an hour and twenty minutes away. I had no time to grab anything other than the kids. I barely had the presence of mind to make sure the stove was off, and the doors were locked.

On the way, I told them what happened, and asked them to pray for their dad. I tried to reassure the kids that their daddy would be okay, and that we had to trust God.

The long drive gave me time to pray. I told God I was trusting Him to be with Jerry and to work out every detail. I reminded God over and over that I was giving this situation to Him to take care of.

When I pulled up at the emergency room I could see the ambulance. Something didn't seem right. They were loading a person onto the ambulance. It looked like the body on the stretcher had a sheet over him.

Was that Jerry?

It couldn't be. The man on the phone said they were taking Jerry to the hospital in Evergreen. He also said Jerry was hurt but was alive.

I couldn't see Jerry's face but had this feeling inside that told me it was him on the stretcher.

I parked the car and told the kids to stay in it. I ran to the ambulance. I identified myself.

When I got closer, I could see the person on the stretcher's face. It was Jerry. The sheet wasn't over him, it just looked like it from a distance.

It still didn't make sense. Why were they loading him in the ambulance?

The ambulance driver told me I had to speak to the ER doctor. She was standing in the doorway of the hospital.

"What's happening?" I asked frantically. "I'm his wife."

"Your husband's bladder exploded and he's bleeding internally. We don't have a surgeon at this hospital. They're taking him to Brewton. They have a surgeon there who can operate on him."

Surgery?

Dear God.

Hadn't we had enough surgeries in our family to last for a lifetime?

"Is my husband going to live?" I asked.

"He's stable, but they need to get him there as soon as possible."

"Thank you."

I started to turn and go back to my car.

"You're lucky you got here when you did," she said. "Due to the new HIPPA laws, I wouldn't have been able to tell you anything."

Apparently, the new HIPPA laws were for privacy and security and had just come out in the spring. Jerry's wreck was in June. She made it seem like if I hadn't shown up in person, I wouldn't have been able to find out any information. They might've not even told me where they were taking him.

God was looking after us and got me there at the perfect time.

I didn't know how to get to Brewton, so I got back in the car and followed the ambulance. As I drove, I told the kids again that every-thing was going to be okay. God had a doctor in Brewton, who was waiting for daddy to operate on his bladder.

Brewton was a thirty-minute drive from Evergreen. After getting to the emergency room, we went straight to the desk. I told them who I was and that my husband had just arrived in the ambulance from Evergreen. The lady said she would check on him and let them know I was in the waiting room.

The lady told me to go to the surgery waiting room. She said the doctor would meet me there after the surgery. While in the waiting room, I called Jerry's mom and dad, gramps and grammy. Since it was getting late, they told me they would get up early and get here as soon as possible.

They had a seven-hour drive. After surgery, they wanted me to call and give them an update on Jerry. I also called a good friend from church, Melinda, and asked her to tell everyone to start praying. Within thirty minutes after hanging up, a sweet older couple from the local church in Brewton came to be with me. Melinda had called the church in Brewton and let them know about Jerry.

The lady asked me if the kids had dinner. When I said they hadn't, they asked if they could take the kids to get something to eat.

"I know we're strangers, but could we take your kids to McDonald's for a happy meal?" one of them said. "It's not far from the hospital."

The kids were hungry. It was after seven and we normally ate dinner at six.

I had no idea how long surgery would take and I wanted to be there when Jerry got out of surgery, so I let the couple take the kids.

At the time, I wasn't even sure I was thinking clearly. Letting my kids leave with strangers. In retrospect, they could've gone to McDonalds and gotten the meals and brought them back to the hospital.

I didn't think of that until they were already gone.

The whole thing was kind of a blur.

But I do remember praying and asking God to keep my kids safe. Even though I didn't know the couple, I could tell that they would be safe with the strangers. Even Caleb. That was the first time I had been apart from him in months.

It felt strange being in a hospital again. Waiting on a surgeon to tell me whether my loved one made it through alive. This time my husband.

How could I live without him?

All kinds of dire thoughts were hitting me all at once. The Bible talks about fiery darts from the enemy. I felt every one of them. My heart felt a pain shoot through it every time I thought about the possibility of facing life without Jerry.

The kids returned from McDonald's and seemed to have a good time. It was probably good that they got away from the hospital for a little while. I thanked the sweet couple for their help. God had sent these angels to take care of my family when I needed it the most.

The wait was longer than I had expected it to be. The surgeon didn't come out until around midnight. As each hour passed, I began to fear the worst.

"How is Jerry doing?" I blurted out, as soon as he walked through the doors into the waiting room.

"He must've had a full bladder when the accident happened," the surgeon said. "The seat belt put pressure on his bladder, and it burst. He was in bad shape. His bladder was shredded, but I was able to put it back together. He also has broken ribs, a broken sternum, and a broken foot, but he will be okay. I'm sending him to the ICU. You can see him in the morning."

I felt a wave of relief wash over me. Although, I wanted to see Jerry tonight. That wasn't possible. I had the kids, and there was no way we could all stay in his room that night.

I thanked the surgeon who seemed to be as exhausted as we were. I told him I'd been praying for him the whole night and that I knew God allowed him to be on call to save my husband. He disappeared behind the doors he'd come out from.

I made a quick call to Jerry's parents. I told them the surgery went well and what the surgeon had told me. I could hear the relief in their voices. I said that Jerry was in ICU, and I could see him at 9:00 a.m.

They'd leave first thing in the morning. I told them to be careful driving, and I would call after seeing him. They thanked me for calling and said it was an answer to their prayers.

I picked up Caleb and woke up Casey and Carly who were sleeping on the waiting room seats. I'd made arrangements to stay at a local hotel. When the surgery dragged into the night, I called them and told the front-desk person we'd be arriving late due to my husband having a car wreck and emergency surgery.

When we arrived, she had everything ready and handed me the key. We were basically there without anything. No clothes other than what we were wearing. No toiletries. Thankfully, the lady gave me four toothbrushes and toothpaste.

I thanked her and we found our room.

I fell into bed exhausted after getting the kids settled.

The next morning, I took the kids to the same McDonalds for breakfast, then we went to the hospital. The kids sat in the waiting room while I went to see Jerry. As soon as I saw his eyes were open, tears started flowing down my face.

I was overwhelmed with gratitude. As soon as I saw him, I knew he was going to be okay. I asked how he was feeling.

"I'm hurting, sore, and it's hard to breathe, but I'm going to be okay."

Jerry couldn't wipe the tears from my cheeks even though I could tell he wanted to.

"I made it to Evergreen just as they were taking you away in the ambulance," I said. "You were covered in a sheet. When I first saw you, I didn't know if you made it. I thought maybe you were dead."

He tried to laugh, but I could tell it hurt too much.

"I'm okay. How are the kids doing?" he asked. Typical Jerry. His first thought was the kids.

"They're in the waiting room. Your mom and dad are on their way to get them and see you. They left early this morning and should be here shortly after lunch."

I asked if he remembered what happened.

"I was going to get off at the next exit to get gas, and I was dying to go to the bathroom. There was a cargo van in front of me, and I couldn't see what happened in front of the van until it was too late. The van swerved into the other lane. A semi-truck was stopped in the middle of the road. I hit the brakes. The next thing I remember is hitting the back of the semi-truck. It was a gas truck, I believe. My car caught on fire."

He took a deep breath.

"God was with me. Somehow, I got my car door cracked. The off-duty policeman who called you pulled me out of the car to a safe area. By then, my car was in flames. The police officer said the gas truck didn't stop right away. Thank God, he drove a little further down the road before pulling over. The gas truck had a safety bar on the bottom of it. Without that bar, I would have gone under the truck. God saved me."

"God's been with you and me every minute," I said. "He provided for us when we needed him the most."

Jerry spent several days in the hospital before being released. Don, Floy, and Marsha, Jerry's sister, made it to the hospital later that day. After seeing Jerry, they took the kids back to Montgomery.

I stayed there with him. I was getting used to spending the days and nights tending to someone in the hospital.

A few days later, Jerry was released. Getting him in the house was extremely difficult and painful. He was able to make it inside with the help of a walker.

I was so thankful he was home. I couldn't stop thanking God for answering my prayers. I knew He was faithful to see us through this difficult situation.

Jerry's favorite dessert is coconut cream pie. He asked if I would make it for him.

"It'll make me feel better. It'll heal me," he said.

He requested that same pie every birthday, and Father's Day.

"Of course, I'll make it for you."

Baking was my happy place. It's where I go when I'm sad or depressed. Feeling lonely or fearful. Even when times are good and I'm filled with joy. In the kitchen, baking a delicious dessert brings me tremendous joy. No matter what is happening around me.

I was pleased to make it for Jerry.

Another added benefit of baking. I love the reaction people have when they eat one of my desserts. It warms my heart to see the satisfaction on their faces.

For a moment, Jerry was able to escape the pain and enjoy a piece of coconut cream pie. On the bottom of the flavorful coconut pastry cream, custard, I add a layer of praline. Pralines go well with coconut, and it adds a crunchy layer to the dessert.

Here is my recipe for Coconut Praline Cream Pie

Coconut Filling

- $1\frac{1}{2}$ cups half and half, divided
- 1 can (13.5 ounce) unsweetened coconut milk, well shaken
- 2 cups sugar
- 6 large egg yolks, lightly beaten
- $\frac{1}{4}$ cup cornstarch
- 4 tablespoons butter
- 3 cups sweetened shredded coconut
- 2 teaspoon pure vanilla
- 1 teaspoon coconut extract

Heat the 1 cup half & half, unsweetened coconut milk, sugar, until slight bubbles. (4 minutes microwave).

In a medium pot, whisk the eggs, cornstarch, ¡ cup half & half.

Temper a cup of warm half and half into the egg mixture.

Add the rest of the half and half.

Whisk constantly until it comes to a slow boil, and thickens, about ten minutes.

Remove the pot from the heat and add the coconut, vanilla, and coconut extract.

Praline Layer

This praline layer is fabulous in coconut pie but goes well in many pies. It will harden as it cools in the bottom of the pie crust.

- 4 tablespoons butter
- 1/3 cup brown sugar
- 1/2 cup pecans

Heat pecans, butter, and brown sugar in a small saucepan until the butter and sugar have dissolved, and mixture begins to boil.

Boil for 30 seconds, then remove from heat.

Pour in the bottom of a deep-dish pie crust that has been pre-baked.

Garnish pie with Whipped topping

- 1 cup heavy whipping cream
- 1/4 cup powdered sugar
- 1 teaspoon coconut extract

Beat whipped cream at high-speed using an electric mixer until foamy. Gradually add the powdered sugar while continuing to beat.

Add the vanilla and beat until stiff peaks form.

Spread or pipe whipped cream over pie filling.

Sprinkle it with toasted coconut.

Try it with your own family. Especially if someone is not feeling well. It does wonders for what ails you.

CHAPTER SIXTEEN

LEAVING ALABAMA

Determining God's Will Is Not Easy

"I'm not moving to Louisiana," I said to Jerry, emphatically. "I told you and God before we were married, I would move anywhere except New Orleans."

I shouldn't have told God that.

Jerry was insistent.

"Diane, I feel like we're being called to move to Louisiana," he said. "They're eliminating my current job and have given me a great job offer. I know you don't want to move to New Orleans, but I feel like God is working on something bigger. Let's go and check out the area. We don't have to live in the city. We can live on the north shore. If we go there and you still don't like it, we won't move."

"I'm not going to like it," I said in a snarky tone. "You already know how I feel about New Orleans. We've only been back in Montgomery for a few years. I love our church, friends, and Alabama which is my home. I'm happy here and don't ever want to leave. This is where I want to raise my kids and grow old."

I'd had a bad experience in New Orleans as a young teenager. Jerry didn't even know about it, because it was a dark secret I'd been keeping deep inside for many years.

When I was fourteen, my family spent the weekend there. This included aunts, uncles, cousins, daddy, and my brother. One Saturday night, a family member wanted to go for a walk, so the whole family joined him. The next thing I knew, we were in the heart of Bourbon Street.

This was a new experience for me. I'd never been around anything like it. I was a small town, Alabama girl. All the activity was a bit overwhelming, and I was out of my element. It made me extremely nervous.

One of my family members led the way. I walked a few feet behind, and the others were behind me. I stayed in the middle because I was afraid that I'd get lost. It was getting late, and the street was full of people. The noise from the bars flooded into the streets along with a number of people who were drunk.

With the large number of people, I fell behind my uncle who was ahead of us. When I turned around, my family wasn't there. I had lost them! They were nowhere in sight.

I thought they must've gone into one of the stores. They probably told me, but I didn't hear them. I looked ahead and all around desperately trying to find a familiar face. My uncle was up ahead, so I ran to him and told him what had happened.

He took my hand and led me further down the street. We went inside one of the many bars that lined the street.

The man at the door stopped my uncle and questioned why a young girl was coming inside.

He told him, "She's with me."

The man motioned us through. I thought that was a little unusual as we continued into the dark, smoky, room. The music was blaring. We sat down, and my uncle ordered a drink. He asked me if I wanted one.

I think he meant alcohol.

I replied, "No, thank you. Nothing for me."

It felt extremely uncomfortable being there. Even at that young an age, I knew we were in a bar and I wasn't supposed to be there. I wasn't old enough to drink. And I hated alcohol and everything associated with it. By that time, I'd already vowed that I'd never drink. And here was my uncle offering me alcohol even though I wasn't legally old enough to drink.

I wanted out of there. I'd lived with my mom Mary's addiction and the problems it caused.

I was scared, nervous, and quiet. Fidgeting. Hoping we would just leave.

The room suddenly got noisy, and a lady appeared on the stage by a pole. She barely had any clothes on and began dancing provocatively to the music. The men in the bar began whooping, whistling, and hollering at the woman.

My uncle sat on the stool staring at the woman. He must've seen my unease with the situation because he tried to reassure me.

"It's okay for you to be here," he said.

I knew differently. If my dad knew my uncle had brought me there, he would've killed him. My dad and uncle never got along anyway. They'd had a running feud for years. My dad tolerated him, but only because he was family.

The lady finished dancing, and my uncle downed the rest of his drink. We went back outside and sat down on a bench. I looked everywhere for the rest of my family.

A few minutes later, they all showed up. They asked what we'd been doing.

"Just sitting here," my uncle replied.

He was such a liar. He never mentioned the strip club and neither did I.

This incident bothered me for a long time. I felt so dirty inside. Like I'd done something wrong. Now I know I didn't. My uncle was the one who should've never taken me to that place.

I kept the secret from my dad until the day he died. If I had told Jerry about it, maybe he would've understood why I was so adamant about not wanting to move to New Orleans.

After I became a Christian, I knew that I needed to forgive my uncle. In reality, I blamed myself. I should've left. I felt like I was old enough to speak up and get out of that situation, but I froze. I'd let fear drive me. I could've found my way back to the hotel but was afraid of venturing out onto the streets of New Orleans alone.

Too many times in my life, I've let fear drive my emotions and weaken my faith. Here I was, years later, still letting that fear control me. What if God did want us to move to New Orleans? Jerry felt so strongly about it.

So, I gave in and we went to New Orleans to check things out. As promised, we spent most of our time on the north shore in Mandeville. There's a twenty-four-mile bridge separating Mandeville from New Orleans, so it didn't even feel like we were in New Orleans.

The whole family went including the kids. On Sunday morning, we all went to church. The family sitting in the seat in front of us had five children. After introducing our family, I found out that the couple had three adopted children.

The lady had started an adoption group in the area and more than a hundred families had adopted children from Eastern Europe. As soon as we met their adoptive children, I felt an impression. A pricking of my spirit. Like the Holy Spirit was speaking to me. Wanting to tell me something.

That God wanted us to adopt a child.

I quickly tamped down that thought. How could I handle any more children with Caleb's medical issues? What if it was a disaster? We were just starting to get things normalized in our own family.

Once again, I was letting fear drive my emotions.

It didn't matter. Surely, I wasn't hearing from the Lord. No one else was hearing it. I'd keep that secret like I'd kept the one from my teenage years.

Up to that point, Carly was adamant that she didn't want to move. Even more so than I was. She loved our church and her friends back home.

After talking to the woman at the church and meeting her adoptive children, Carly blurted out, "It's probably God's will for us to move here. If we don't, we might be missing out on His plans for us. Mom, God wants you to adopt a sister for me."

I about fell off the pew.

But did manage a quick comeback.

"I hate to disappoint you," I told Carly, "I don't think we're supposed to adopt another child. Your brother's medical issues are all I can handle."

We went home having had a good time. The trip got me thinking. I still didn't want to move, but I kept feeling like it might be the right thing to do.

Jerry's job offer was a good one. My kids should experience new things. I barely left Alabama as a kid. That might be why I feared big cities.

Maybe God was going to redeem my bad experience in New Orleans.

After a lot of prayerful consideration, Jerry took the job, and our house sold in three weeks. Another sign from God. We moved out of our home the day before Thanksgiving. We didn't want to move the kids to New Orleans until school was out for Christmas, so we moved into a hotel for a couple of weeks.

To complicate things, Caleb had an episode and we had to rush him to Atlanta for emergency surgery. Fortunately, it wasn't a prolonged situation. He was released from the hospital a few days later.

A lot of things hit us at once during that time. As if moving wasn't traumatic enough, Marsha, Jerry's sister, had surgery for breast cancer, the same day as Caleb's shunt surgery. Hers was successful as well, but she had to start six months of chemo right afterwards.

While we were in Atlanta for Caleb's surgery, we received a call from Jerry's mom, Floy. She was upset. We figured it had to do with Marsha and some complication related to her surgery. Turns out, Uncle Charles had a horrible accident at the stockyard in Cookeville. A large cow picked him up by its horns and tossed him into a pole. He had to be airlifted to Erlanger Hospital in Chattanooga.

Jerry left Atlanta immediately for Chattanooga to be with his cousins and aunt during this horrible time. Caleb was out of the hospital by that time, and I stayed back to rest in the hotel in Montgomery while Casey and Carly were finishing school. Life was crazy, but I was thankful for the rest.

Jerry called from Erlanger with bad news. I could tell from the tone of his voice he was upset.

"Uncle Charles didn't make it," he said.

This wasn't the uncle who'd taken me to the strip bar in New Orleans. Uncle Charles was fun-loving and always made everyone laugh. We had a special bond talking about desserts. He loved sweets as much as I did. I would tell him all about the cakes and pies I baked, and he would listen intently. At Christmas time, he was the first to the dessert table. He piled his plate full like it was his main course.

He was a hard-working, thin built farmer who never worried about his weight.

Our moving plans had to be put on hold as Jerry wanted us all to come to Cookeville for Uncle Charles' funeral.

Our house wasn't ready anyway. Two days before Christmas, we heard from our builder in Mandeville. Due to excessive rain, our house wouldn't be ready for another three or four weeks. I was mentally calculating the cost of another month in a hotel. We needed to get the kids in their new school in Louisiana, plus I was anxious to get a place to settle for a while. After telling us the bad news, the builder invited us to stay in his corporate townhouse.

That wasn't the last of the complications, but eventually we laid Uncle Charles to rest and got our family moved to Louisiana.

* * *

My love of cooking and baking exploded in Louisiana. Growing up in South Alabama, we ate a lot of seafood. My dad, his friends, and my brothers would go fresh and salt-water fishing. They would catch catfish, bass, flounder, shrimp, crawfish, and even crabs. We grew up with little money but enjoyed delicious fried fish and hushpuppies, shrimp, or crawfish boils weekly.

So I fit right in with the Louisiana food scene.

It was there that I learned to develop a depth of flavor with the Cajun cooking trinity (onion, bell pepper, and celery), and the spices used commonly in Louisiana.

One of the highlights was that Caleb and I met celebrity Chef Paul Prudhomme who was famous for using the trinity and Cajun Spices. Chef Paul owned K-Paul's, a famous New Orleans Cajun and Creole restaurant.

Before starting K-Paul's, Chef Paul worked at the famous Commander's Palace as head chef. Emeril Lagasse became head chef after Chef Paul. Paul Prudhomme did a cooking demonstration at a local grocery store for their grand opening. Caleb and I got there early to stand in the front row.

I had admired Chef Paul, but even more so after meeting him. He took time to talk to Caleb and even invited him to help stir his dish. He made a pasta recipe with andouille sausage, shrimp, and fettuccini. It also had bell pepper, celery, onion, and spices. Caleb thought he was something special getting to help the famous chef and beamed like a lighthouse while stirring the dish.

I listened intently as Chef Paul explained his recipe. After the demonstration, Chef Paul spent more time talking to Caleb and me. I was able to ask him questions about his love of cooking. He told me it came from his momma who loved being in the kitchen and trying new things. He encouraged me to try experimenting in the kitchen.

Beaming with excitement, I couldn't wait to fix some new recipes. I fell in love with making Crawfish Pie, Barbecued Shrimp, Cajun Shrimp Alfredo, and Cajun Potato Salad, to name a few. I enjoyed cooking Cajun food, but my favorite was baking Cajun desserts. I practiced making White Chocolate Bread Pudding, Crème Brule, Pralines, Banana Foster, Creole Style Cheesecake and more. Homemade sauces like Praline, Caramel, and Crème Anglaise became my favorite go-to.

It was a major influence in the dishes I made in competitions years later.

One day, I took Caleb to watch Emeril Lagasse do a live cooking demonstration. At the time, Emeril had a cooking show on Food Network. Emeril Live was Caleb's favorite T.V. show. He giggled over and over every time Emeril said, "Bam!"

Although we did not get a chance to talk to Emeril, it was still awesome to see Caleb with his mouth wide open in "awe" of him.

Meeting Chef Paul Prudhomme, watching Emeril Lagasse and living in Louisiana, and eating the best food I had ever had, inspired me to be creative in the kitchen and have fun cooking.

The whirlwind of cooking caused me to forget what Carly had said about moving to New Orleans.

"God wants us to move there so you can adopt a sister for me."

I may have forgotten, but God hadn't.

CHAPTER SEVENTEEN

OVERCOMING ADOPTION HEARTACHES

He dropped ten orphans at my door.

Carly is the spiritual discerner in the family. I've always been sensitive to spiritual things as well, but Carly has this uncanny knack for hearing God's will for our family in the most remarkable ways.

She was the one who said we were going to have twins before a doctor had confirmed it.

I wouldn't have believed it except that Casey and Caleb were born a year or so after she prophesied it.

She was at it again. Before we moved to New Orleans, she had insisted God wanted us to move to Louisiana and adopt a girl, so that she'd have a sister. It was easy to pass it off as the fantasy of a young girl and her imagination.

I figured she'd eventually forget about it. Instead, she kept mentioning it. Part of it had come true. We did move to the New Orleans area. We saw the mother with the adopted children every Sunday, so it was hard not to be reminded.

"Mom and Dad, I've been praying you will adopt me a baby sister," Carly said for the umpteenth time.

"Carly," I explained, "you can pray, but God is going to have to show me it's His will for our lives. I'm exhausted from having the three kids I have already."

Since she was so certain, I did begin to pray about it too. My prayer went something like, "Lord, you know I have my hands full with three children. You also know Caleb has unique needs and requires a shunt to keep him alive. Now's not the right time for another baby."

Thanks, but no thanks. Having another child to take care of seemed like the last thing I wanted.

Caleb's shunt had failed seventeen times requiring life or death surgery every time. He had brain damage and required constant care and attention. I barely had a moment to myself.

"Lord, how can I handle another child? Especially a child who doesn't even speak English and lives halfway across the world."

It didn't seem possible anyway. Certainly, it wasn't God's will since there were so many obstacles in the way. How could I ever leave Caleb long enough to go overseas and meet one of the children? Who would watch him? What if he had a shunt failure while I was gone?

Caleb still couldn't communicate with others. I'd been around him so much that we could read each other's thoughts, but I still didn't always know when he was in pain. He hid things so well. Probably because he knew if I knew he was hurting it might mean he'd have to go back to the hospital and endure more suffering.

My husband wasn't in a position to take on another mouth to feed financially. Having another mouth to feed and adding that pressure didn't seem wise.

I barely had enough time for Jerry now. What would it be like with another child?

"Jerry needs me, Lord. His job requires him to be out of town, several nights a week. How could I handle another child without him here to help me? How could we afford it?"

I went on and on. Voicing every excuse under the sun. Everything I could think of as to why we couldn't adopt.

Finally, I said, "If it's your plan for our family, God, you'll have to drop an orphan at my door. In fact, drop more than one. Several, actually. Otherwise, I won't believe you're the one behind it."

I figured that closed the matter. I certainly wasn't going to pursue it. I'd thrown down my fleece. God would have to do the impossible and give us multiple children to adopt, if he wanted to get my attention.

Sigh.

I should've known not to test God.

* * *

Several months went by, and in April 2005, the same lady at church with the five adoptive children asked Jerry and me if we would like to host an orphan. The adoption group had raised enough funds to bring ten orphans to America.

Ten!

"We can't host ten orphans," I said.

"You don't have to host all ten. Just one," she explained.

That was a relief. That I could do. We weren't adopting a child. Just hosting one for a couple of weeks. It seemed like a good way to dip the proverbial toe in the water.

After talking to Jerry, we agreed to take in one of the orphans. I started reading every book I could find on hosting orphans and adoption.

During that process, I could feel my heart shifting. I learned how important orphans were to God. The Bible even commands Christians to take care of the orphans. Confirmation we were doing the right thing by hosting the one child. It warmed my heart to know we were doing something important to God.

"Religion that God our Father accepts as pure and faultless is this: to look after orphans and widows in their distress and to keep oneself from being polluted by the world."
(James 1:27 NIV)

My heart was also softening towards adoption. The Bible says we have been adopted by God. I read the many verses. God adopted us as a part of His family through the blood of Jesus. Adopting a child, and giving him a future and hope, painted a beautiful picture of what the Lord did for us in welcoming us into His family. He gives us hope of a future with Him in heaven one day.

Millions of orphans don't have a chance to grow up in a Christian home and may not even know God. How could they come to know God unless someone like Jerry and I sacrificed and gave them a home? Not only give them a family and the love that they need but let them know about God and Jesus and what He's done for us.

A major shift was happening. Rather than resisting adoption, I was actually becoming excited about it.

What about all my excuses? The obstacles still remained. But I'd learned that if I am doing something God has told me to do, He will take care of the details.

Little did I know that God was working behind the scenes. He was waiting for me to join Him in putting the plan in place. Jerry was becoming excited about it as well. My husband and daughter already understood God was calling us to adopt, and they were working on me.

It still didn't feel like the timing was right. My life was stressful enough. I was exhausted all the time. How could I take on more kids?

We agreed to take on the one boy. Temporarily. Nothing about it was permanent. Everyone was excited about it. Especially Caleb. He didn't really know what it all meant, but he could tell something exciting was happening in our family.

I tried to temper everyone's enthusiasm. Warned them to not get too attached. We weren't adopting this boy. We were hosting him. Besides, Carly said we were going to give her a sister. It couldn't be God's will that we adopt a boy.

On the way to the airport to meet the boy for the first time, we got a phone call.

"Diane, I am so sorry," the lady on the line said. "The little boy who was coming to stay with you didn't get on the airplane. He woke up with chickenpox yesterday and wasn't able to come. Only nine kids got on the plane."

We were crushed.

Tears were actually shed. We'd never met the young boy, but it felt like a loss.

What should we do? Turn around and go home or go on to the airport and meet the other nine children. They were already placed with other families. It seemed like it might be too hard if we left there without a child after seeing the other kids.

As a family, we decided to go and greet the other orphans.

I'm glad we did. It was so fun. One by one, the kids were introduced to their host families. When they first got off the plane, their heads were down, and they were clearly nervous.

They soon began to warm to everyone and give out hugs.

We took pictures of the kids and their host families and showed each child their picture on the screen on our camera.

They loved it!

The kids took turns taking pictures. Seeing the pictures through the display screen caused huge smiles to come on their faces. My family and I were still disappointed, but at the same time, we were thrilled for the other orphans and their host families.

We volunteered the following evening to host the two orphanage workers who chaperoned the kids to America. During the dinner and through an interpreter, the orphanage workers shared their concerns. They were worried about the children being scattered all over New Orleans in different homes with a hurricane looming in the Gulf.

They asked us to host all the children for a couple of days.

"What does that mean?" I asked.

"We'd like it if you'd keep all nine kids here at your house."

We said "yes" without any hesitation. God blessed us with, not one, but nine orphans ages seven to ten years old for two days.

Nine kids. I'd told God he had to give me more than one for me to believe he wanted us to adopt.

Was this the answer to my fleece?

Was God showing out His sense of humor?

I'd put the impossible on Him. "Give me several orphans," I said to God almost sarcastically.

We had nine in our house at one time!

It didn't feel like a burden at all. We fell in love with those kids. It brought me great joy to see them grinning from ear to ear. We flipped pancakes, baked homemade cookies and pizza, watched Disney movies, played with our dogs, ate ice cream and candy, and swam. It's the first time most of those kids had done any of those things.

The hurricane turned out to be nothing. God spared us from Hurricane Dennis. It made landfall on the Florida panhandle as a category three hurricane. It missed us entirely so the kids were able to stay with us the whole time and were perfectly safe.

While the orphans were in our house, God was working on my heart. One morning, I opened our bedroom door to find a seven-year-old boy cuddled up in a ball on the floor next to our door. The little boy, Valery, jumped up and gave Jerry and me the biggest hug. Later, I found out from the translator that he had slept there all-night waiting for us to come out.

I remembered my prayer.

If you want me to adopt, you'll drop an orphan at my door.

At the time, I meant the front door, but that was being a little too pedantic. The bedroom door was a door as well.

Seeing that boy solidified it for me. I knew beyond a shadow of a doubt that God was calling our family to adopt.

The translator said, "They all want to be loved so badly."

At that point, I was ready to adopt all of them.

Each night, we would tuck the children in bed. Valery would wrap his arms around my neck and give me a big hug every time. He kept hugging me and would tell me in English that he loved me.

The boy pulled on my heartstrings like a puppet master pulls on the strings of his marionette.

God used those precious children to prepare us for adoption. He taught us the true meaning and what all would be involved. We saw how much they needed us. Each one of them was hungry for love and attention.

When the children left to spend the rest of the time with their host families, we were sad but so thankful we had them even for a short time. We were also physically exhausted. We not only had the children, but all the host families were in and out all weekend.

Although we were tired, we were the blessed ones. We would remember that weekend forever.

Two days later, Valery came back to stay with us. His host family had a small child who was jealous of him, and it wasn't a good situation. We were asked if we would mind hosting him the remainder of the time. Of course, our family agreed.

Valery was sensitive, funny, and happy while staying at our home. Within a day, he was back to telling us he loved us. *I love you* were his first English words.

When the time came for the children to go back home, we had to be at the airport at 11:00 am. As I put Valery's clothes in his suitcase, he took the clothes out of it. I knew this would be difficult for our family, but I had no idea how hard it would be for him to say goodbye.

Without speaking any English, he made it clear he wanted to stay. I picked up his clothes from the bed he had taken out of his suitcase, folded them, and placed them back in the luggage. He again took everything out as soon as I put it in.

Jerry distracted Valery while I packed his suitcase and put it in the car. Once at the airport, the orphanage workers talked to him about going home. It was a sad day for all of us. As I stood there waving goodbye, with tears streaming down my face, I asked God to allow these children to be adopted into a loving Christian home.

After the orphans left, we had a family meeting. We decided to start the long adoption process. That meant filling out dossiers. We called the adoption agency to check on the status of Valery. We were devastated to find out that a family in Georgia was planning on adopting him. They had already scheduled their first trip overseas to see him.

After this roller coaster of emotions, we decided to adopt two older siblings. By adopting siblings, we could get a boy and a girl—the sister

Carly always wanted. Most families only wanted a baby or one child. We found out siblings and older children were challenging to place. We felt like God was leading us to adopt older children who might not ever get a chance to know about Him.

Adopting would require us to make several overseas trips. Leaving Caleb for that long required me to put all my faith in God. During one of Caleb's emergency surgeries, I had told Jerry I would never leave Caleb. But if God was calling us to adopt, I would have to trust Him with all my heart. I knew leaving Caleb would be the hardest thing I would ever do.

We prayed, "God, please allow us to make each adoption trip without Caleb having shunt failure. Please close all doors if we are not meant to go down this road. We need to hear from you before making any decisions."

Of course, nothing seemed to come easy for our family. Adopting was no exception. We'd have to overcome numerous obstacles. But we were determined.

CHAPTER EIGHTEEN
HURRICANE KATRINA

Storms raged around us.

August 2005

Life is sometimes filled with storms. There are the valleys of the shadow of death as the Psalmist said. But by definition, if there are valleys, there are also mountaintops. Those times when things are going well. When life has extended periods of joy.

We've had our share of both. Good times and bad. In this memoir, I don't want to leave you with the impression that life has always been hard. The purpose of this book is to share those difficult times with you, mostly so you'd understand the process the Lord led me through to become totally dependent on Him.

Hopefully, that will encourage you to learn that truth faster than I did.

My life has been a roller coaster of trials and emotions. Every time bad things would happen, I'd spiral into unbelief and fear. Then God would somehow help me through the hard times and my faith would be strengthened.

For years, I asked why. At some point, I quit asking. In August 2005, I was still in the miry clay of questioning.

Why do bad things keep happening to us?

We hadn't been in Louisiana that long. Things were looking up. Caleb was better. Jerry liked his new job, and it brought in enough money to meet our needs. My cooking blossomed as I learned Cajun dishes and my repertoire of skills were expanding. The kids were doing well in school. We had a good church and were developing lifelong friendships. We had even started the adoption process.

The calm before the literal storm so to speak.

Another hurricane had formed in the Gulf of Mexico. Hurricane Katrina.

The whole town was talking about it and it's all we heard about on the news. Jerry and I woke up early one August morning and watched the latest reports.

"It's headed toward New Orleans," the weatherman said.

Casey and Caleb's ninth birthday party had been scheduled at Mandeville Sports Complex at 10:00 am that morning. Jerry and I wondered if we should cancel. It seemed premature to do so. Hurricanes were unpredictable. It could easily swerve and miss us. Even if it didn't, we had a couple of days to prepare.

We decided to go to the party and see if anyone showed up. If not, we would simply return home and finish our preparations. Even though they hadn't yet called for a mandatory evacuation, we started preparing to leave. Since we had several hours before the party, we got a lot done before we left for the complex. We carried everything from the backyard that had the potential to blow away and stored it in the garage and began packing.

On the way to the birthday party, we stopped to fill up with gas. We weren't the only ones preparing to leave. The gas lines were long. We waited for a long time, but eventually got our gas and then drove to the Sports Complex.

Within minutes, people started showing up for the party. All the kids invited were able to attend. That was a relief. I was concerned the boys would be disappointed if no one showed. The kids played while the parents talked about what we needed to do before evacuating and where we were going and what we were all doing.

Even though we were stressed about the hurricane, the boys had a great birthday.

After the party, we went home to continue preparing to evacuate. Jerry made several trips to get sandbags. We sandbagged our home and boarded up the windows. Then we packed our bin of essential documents, gathered the scrapbooks full of family pictures, and got enough clothes for a couple of weeks for everyone.

I put all our frozen food in trash bags. I didn't want to come home to a mess and horrible stench if we lost power and all the meat thawed. I'm the type of person who plans for the worst and hopes for the best.

Hurricane Katrina was not my first hurricane. My earliest childhood memory was when I was four years old. I remembered my father getting ready for Hurricane Camille in Mobile, Alabama.

Camille made landfall along the Mississippi Gulf Coast as a category five hurricane late in the evening on August 17, 1969. In preparation, we took everything off the walls, filled trash bags with our frozen foods, then placed the bags back into the freezer.

Dad worked across the street from our home in a cinder block building. We gathered up as many blankets and pillows as we could and carried them across the street. Daddy made my two brothers, sister, and me a pallet in the middle of the floor. The room had a steel door with no windows in it.

"We'll be safe in here," he had said. "Everything will be okay."

I fell asleep that night knowing I was safe with daddy around.

The next day, trees were down everywhere. Daddy reassured us everything was going to be okay and told us the hurricane missed us but was bad in Mississippi. For whatever reason, I wasn't scared. I guess having my dad there was what calmed my nerves.

The impending hurricane in Louisiana was a different story. My dad had already passed, and I was feeling the anxiety not having him around to reassure me. A thousand questions were swirling around in my mind like the hurricane had already hit me mentally and emotionally on the inside.

What if the hurricane destroys our house?

Where would we live?

What if the house survived, but we were without power?

What if the roads were impassable and we couldn't get home?

What if the stores were closed and we didn't have access to food and water?

What if Caleb had an episode? Would the hospitals be open? Could we even get to them?

What if ... What if ... What if ...

My thoughts were out of control.

That's why I insisted on making so many preparations. Staying busy took my mind off the impending disaster I was already convinced was coming. A lot of people were staying behind to ride it out. That wasn't an option for us. We were getting out of there as soon as possible and I wanted to take as many precautions as we could and hope we didn't need them.

My dad was over prepared when the hurricane hit in 1969, and all the trouble we went to was for nothing. He didn't care. He told us it was better to be over prepared than underprepared.

That's where I got it from.

As I packed the freezer in our house, I prayed and asked God to protect our home. Sometimes it took me a while, but eventually I got around to calling on God. After hours, sometimes days of worrying.

Even with my prayers, I still had an uneasy feeling about things.

By Saturday evening, a mandatory evacuation was called for St. Tammany Parish which was where we lived. We made plans to leave by 5:00 am on Sunday, August 28, which was actually the boys' ninth birthday.

Because the traffic was so bad, we decided to leave during the early morning hours. Jerry searched for a hotel but was unable to find one within a few hours of our home. We wanted to find a hotel an hour or two inland so we could make it back home in case we needed to put a tarp on our house. If we were close by, we might have a chance to get back into the city before the streets were blocked off.

We ended up with a reservation in Marksville, Louisiana at a casino-hotel which was the only thing available. The plans were set. At five a.m., we'd leave the house behind and hope for the best.

That night, the kids slept well, but Jerry and I didn't. Hopefully, the kids felt what I felt as a child. Safe knowing their dad and mom would protect them. Jerry and I tried to keep each other calm, but we were glued to the TV as Katrina got stronger and moved closer to New Orleans.

The news people were sensationalizing the threat. They talked about the worst-case scenarios over and over again.

"It's not looking good," I told Jerry, as I watched too much of the news.

"We have to trust God to take care of us," Jerry said. "We have prepared everything we can and have prayed about it several times. Try to get some sleep."

I couldn't sleep thinking about what else I could do. In the middle of the night, I woke Jerry and asked him to let more water out of the pool. He was tired and frustrated with me.

"I've worked all day," he said. "I'm exhausted! We must trust God to do the rest."

I was tired and weary too. The fear of losing everything was overwhelming, but I knew Jerry was right. I continued to pray and give God my worries. He was the only one who could really help us. I had to find peace in the middle of this storm raging around me and inside me. I continued praying until I fell asleep.

When the time came, I woke the kids. My little Carly was organized and ready to go. Her clothes were on her bed, her suitcase packed, and her backpack with school books ready. Carly was always super organized and helpful. After a hug, and telling her everything was going to be okay, I went to the boys' room.

I tried to wake them up with a cheery surprise. "Good morning, Casey and Caleb! Happy Birthday, boys! Get dressed. We're leaving soon."

I tried to make it sound fun.

"We'll eat a birthday lunch at the hotel buffet when we get there. I've got your favorite snacks in the car."

Their clothes were already packed and ready to go. We'd finished that task the night before. All they had to do was get dressed, brush their teeth, and get out to the car.

I gave them both big reassuring hugs. Out of the blue, Caleb went over to Casey and hugged his brother. Maybe his way of saying Happy Birthday. Or possibly Caleb sensed that something was wrong. He couldn't possibly know what, but he had to know that something was different in our routine. We didn't usually get up that early in the morning.

After Caleb hugged his brother, he walked around his room like he was in some kind of daze. Clearly confused and trying to figure things out. I knelt on the floor in front of him.

"Caleb, we're going to a hotel for a few days. You can go swimming, and they have a lot of good food."

Caleb loves to eat and swim. I could see the excitement on his face and knew he was better. After another hug, I pointed him to the bathroom, where I already had his toothbrush ready for him to brush his teeth. Putting his toothpaste on his toothbrush was nearly impossible with his cerebral palsy, so I followed him in to help him.

We met our friends at five that morning and headed to Marksville. The traffic was heavy but not horrible. We arrived in Marksville around ten. Our friends' parents happened to live there. We were able to stay with them until we checked into our hotel, and they also kept our dogs for a couple of days.

After checking into the hotel, we went downstairs to find the buffet for a late birthday lunch. I grabbed my boys' hands and walked as fast as I could. We had to pass through the casino to get to the buffet. It was loud, and dinging noises were going off everywhere.

Casey kept saying over and over, "We're in a casino! We're in a casino!"

He was saying it to push my buttons, and I tried my best to ignore him. He knew I didn't feel comfortable there with the small children.

Even though we had just arrived, I was already exhausted, stressed, and ready to go home. I managed to control my tongue because I didn't want to ruin the kids' birthday by complaining. One thing important to me was that I wanted my kids to have great memories of their birthdays. My goal on each of them was for kids to have no doubt they were loved.

Growing up I couldn't remember having a good birthday, nor being told by my mother she loved me. I can't remember one mother's hug on a birthday. She never baked me a birthday cake or got me a present. I didn't want the chaos around us this year to cause me to react in a negative way leaving a horrible birthday memory for my kids.

We made it to the restaurant, where we found an excellent seafood buffet, including crab legs, which the boys loved. The desserts were fabulous. After seeing my favorite desserts, including luscious chocolate cake, white chocolate bread pudding, cheesecake with fudge topping, and chocolate chip cookies, I knew God was trying to tell me everything was going to be okay.

The waitstaff surprised us when they handed Casey and Caleb a colossal ice cream sundae with whipped cream and a cherry on top. They gathered around and started singing "Happy Birthday."

I thanked God for showing up, even in a casino. God blessed us with a wonderful birthday meal for our boys. We went back to the room to turn on the TV again, which we were glued to for the next several days.

The eye of Katrina went over Slidell, Louisiana. Initially, it was good for New Orleans. Everyone thought New Orleans had been spared since it didn't take a direct hit. We found out quickly it could not have been worse for New Orleans. Not only was the rain heavy, but the wind circled counterclockwise and dumped water from Lake Pontchartrain into New Orleans. The extreme amount of water caused stress on the levees and pumps. The pumps eventually broke. New Orleans quickly filled up with water, and the city flooded. Levees broke all over the city.

In some areas, only rooftops were visible. We watched helicopters rescue people from their rooftops and boats trying to rescue others. Jerry and our friend decided as soon as Katrina passed, that they would go back to Mandeville to see if they could help anyone and check the status of our homes.

They got up early on August 30th and set off not knowing what they might find. The roads were already barricaded, and they had to prove they lived in the neighborhood to even enter. Thank God, our house was virtually untouched. The only issue was five huge, uprooted trees that had fallen within inches of our home and Jerry couldn't get in the driveway.

The neighbor's house to our left wasn't as fortunate. They had a huge tree that divided their home in half. We knew they planned on riding out the storm. Jerry made sure they were okay and helped put tarps on their roofs. Our friend did the same with his neighbors and extended family's homes.

The power was out in most of south Louisiana, including Mandeville. Businesses and schools were closed. Because of the extensive damage, no one had any idea when things would be open. It looked like it was going to be a long while before we would return home.

Things were even worse in New Orleans which had extensive damage all over the city. Eighty percent of the city was underwater. Lots of people lived on the North Shore of New Orleans in Mandeville, Madisonville, and the Covington area. They commuted to work in New Orleans across a twenty-four-mile bridge. Unfortunately, it would be a long time before things could get back to normal.

Back at the casino, I tried to keep the kids' routines as normal as possible. We went swimming and played in the room. Went outside when we could, while keeping an eye on the television and the tragedy unfolding in New Orleans.

Jerry returned with news that the house wasn't damaged but unlivable for now. We'd just have to wait it out. He tried to work from our hotel in Marksville, but that was hard on him. At some point, we realized the situation wasn't workable and decided to drive to Gainsboro, Tennessee, over seven hundred miles away, to stay with Grammy and Gramps for a few days.

Even that trip wasn't without challenges. Gas shortages were everywhere. The lines to get gas were longer than I'd ever seen. At some stations, hundreds of cars tried to fill up. In other places, lines of cars backed up to the interstate as they waited for gas. Because we were on the road again before 6:00 a.m., we were able to get gas before getting on the interstate with no wait.

We thanked God we were able to get gas, especially since we'd heard the night before, that the stations had run entirely out of gasoline. They'd gotten a shipment in during the night.

God was taking care of us. We were relieved to get to Tennessee safely and thankful to have a place to wash loads of dirty clothes and rest and I had some help with the kids.

That lasted for several days. Jerry had work to do in Tyler, Texas, and wanted us to go with him. So, we packed up the kids and made the long drive to Texas. He visited customers during the day while I stayed at the hotel with the kids.

I could tell things were starting to weigh on them. For a while, it was fun to swim in the hotel pool and pretend we were on vacation. After a few days, we all longed for home. They even mentioned they missed school, their church, and friends.

I didn't know what to tell them. I didn't know how long it'd be before we could return home. I searched for information about expected dates for electricity coming back on and schools reopening. One was in private school and two were in public school. Both schools hoped to start back in a few weeks, depending on electricity getting back on by then, but they couldn't set a specific date.

The schools were concerned about teachers and students not returning because of damage to their homes or parents losing their jobs in New Orleans. Many families had at least one parent who worked in New Orleans. Who knew if they'd even still have a job after the mess was cleared.

Getting everything reopened was going to take a while. A month after Hurricane Katrina hit, we still didn't have electricity at our house.

I felt so unsettled with things still up in the air.

Then we got the news that another hurricane was headed for New Orleans. Hurricane Rita was churning in the gulf.

I panicked. I sat on the floor, crying, and begging God to let Rita completely miss the New Orleans area.

Another disaster was looming.

The water in New Orleans was almost gone after hurricane Katrina hit. The restoration was beginning, including getting electricity turned back on in parts of the city and surrounding areas.

What would happen if we got another direct hit?

At that time, we had traveled to Little Rock, Arkansas, for Jerry's work. That Friday we planned to go to Memphis and then finally go home on Saturday to see if we had power or not. We had to put those plans on hold. We stayed in Memphis and waited to see what Rita would bring.

Hurricane Rita hit the Louisiana and Texas border. Parts of New Orleans flooded again from all the rain Rita brought with it. We watched in horror as the entire nightmare scenario repeated itself. We weren't particularly worried about our house, but more about the turmoil the new storm would cause. The setback to our time frame.

When would we be able to go home?

I couldn't stand living out of a suitcase. Not being able to cook for my family. Not even able to bake them a dessert.

Now I was second guessing our decision to move to begin with. It put a strain on our marriage. Everyone could feel the stress. I was so frustrated. I thought my head was going to explode.

I talked to Jerry about wanting to move. From that day forward, I prayed daily for God to open a door for us to move away from the coast.

To make matters worse, Jerry started drinking again.

Hospitals were closed in South Louisiana from hurricane damage, which meant Jerry lost a lot of business since he sold capital equipment to them. My gut told me he was drinking again, so I confronted him about it.

"I know you're stressed," I said. "But please don't relapse. You told me to trust God, and you need to do the same thing."

I was so angry at Jerry. He was always telling me to trust God but now he was running from God himself. Using alcohol to cope with all the stress. Normally, Jerry was the positive one who looked for the good in everything. This time he was letting everything get the best of him.

How was I supposed to hold everything together? Didn't he know that drinking would only make things worse?

All we could do was continue to endure the trial.

Eventually, the power was turned back on, and schools did reopen, and we were able to return home. Things were not the same though.

Businesses were destroyed. People lost their jobs. There were constant shortages of supplies. Food. It took months for shelves to be restocked.

Sadly, houses were going up for sale all around us. We lost neighbors and friends who couldn't return because of damage to their homes or lost jobs.

We were some of the lucky ones in the sense that our home wasn't damaged, and Jerry still had his job.

That's sort of how things were for me, I was realizing. I went through these horrible tragic situations, but somehow came out of them with things not being as bad as they could've been. I attribute that to God watching out for us.

Then one of my worst fears came to pass.

"Caleb, are you okay?" I had asked one day.

He didn't answer. He sat on the floor and leaned on the couch, rooting his head on the sofa.

I knelt beside him. "Caleb, do you have a headache?" I asked.

Again, no answer. I lifted him on the couch to sit beside me. Caleb leaned over and rooted his head on me. My heart sank. I tried to calmly get Jerry's attention.

"I need to call the neurosurgeon," I said.

Jerry knew what I was talking about, but Caleb also knew.

Caleb raised his head and shook his head violently from side to side. Because of all his shunt complications in the past, he feared hospitals and doctors.

"We have to go see if your shunt is working," I explained. "If we don't, it's only going to get worse."

I called everywhere. The Children's Hospital in New Orleans was closed due to flooding. I called to see if Caleb's neurosurgeon was working somewhere else. None of the neurosurgeons were. The woman on the phone told me to take Caleb to the closest emergency room.

Alabama was obviously out of the question. It'd take hours to get there.

I couldn't believe this was happening.

We survived hurricane Katrina but now I was worried our son was going to die. We called every hospital we could think of to see if they were open and if they had a neurosurgeon available. Call after call, I was told no.

My stomach was churning and I feared the worst.

All I knew to do was pray.

What good would that do? If Caleb didn't get to a hospital, he would die.

But I prayed anyway. As hard as I knew how to pray. I've since learned that my prayers were somewhat misguided. We don't have to beg God to help us. He wants to. In fact, he responds to our faith. Even though I wasn't getting the words right, and I was praying out of fear, I'm thankful that God answered my prayers without judgment.

Caleb was able to keep his pain medicine down. For the first time ever after a migraine. Caleb seemed to be getting better without needing surgery. We thought maybe his slit ventricles were causing the shunt not to drain enough but started working better. I would've loved to have a neurosurgeon's opinion but was comforted by the thought that his symptoms seemed to be getting better.

God answered our prayers and Caleb was okay without having to endure a surgery.

We survived a hurricane and another medical scare.

What else could life throw at me? Bring it on. I can handle it.

The thought occurred to me.

I guess I really can survive anything with God's help.

CHAPTER NINETEEN
ADOPTION DAY

God loves His children no matter what.

Our adoption process was put on hold for the longest time. After Hurricane Katrina, Eastern Europe wasn't allowing adoptions into Louisiana. They weren't even accepting dossiers.

Jerry and I discussed it and prayed about what to do. We decided to continue with the process. Carly would be going to college soon and desperately wanted a sister. Her proclamation that we were going to adopt a girl was also in the back of our minds.

If God closed the door, it'd mean it wasn't His will for us. Since we all believe it was God's will, we'd pursue it until we were out of options. Like seemingly everything else in my life, perseverance was required. I'd certainly had enough experience with troubles not to give up just because of a few setbacks.

Hurricane Katrina had flooded the Homeland Security building, so a year later, we still hadn't been approved to adopt children from a foreign country. Our fingerprints, background checks, and citizenship paperwork for the children had to be resubmitted.

Over a year later, we finally received an approval letter from homeland security. I opened the correspondence with great anticipation.

We were approved!

It'd taken so long I wasn't sure it was ever going to happen.

Something was wrong with the letter, though. They misspelled my name. DenisDiana Roark, instead of Diane Roark.

What did that mean? Did we have to start the whole process over again? Where did Denis come from? Would we have to wait another year?

We were so frustrated.

Were we wasting our time anyway? We didn't even know if we'd be allowed to adopt. The children might not be available for adoption. It's possible we were getting our hopes up for nothing. It sure felt like a closed door.

Would it be this hard if God was really behind it? So many questions reared their ugly heads during this time of waiting.

We still continued to pray and be patient.

In March of 2006, we received a referral for two children from our adoption agency. A brother and sister. My heart jumped and did several somersaults when we were notified. It seemed like things were finally moving in the right direction.

I'd been hesitant at first to adopt children. Once I decided to do it, the anticipation started building inside of me. As time passed, the desire kept growing. Like a volcano about to erupt.

It finally looked like it was going to happen. In the approval letter, it said their names were Denis and Diana.

Sound familiar?

Jerry caught it right away.

The names were the same as the misspelled names on the Homeland Security approval letter!

DenisDiana Roark.

How was that possible?

That couldn't be a coincidence. Only God could do something that miraculous. It had to be a sign.

"God spelled it out for you," Jerry said with a huge smile on his face. "How much clearer does He need to be? Our children are Denis and Diana."

He was right. Those were our children. I knew it in my heart.

* * *

Somewhere over the Atlantic Ocean

"Diane, why are you so quiet?" Jerry asked me. "What are you thinking about?"

We were on an airplane flying to meet our new children. We had little information about them. All we knew was that they were a boy and a girl who lived in an orphanage in Romania and their names were Denis and Diana. We had no background information at all.

The reason for the trip was to meet the kids and make a final decision about adopting them. We couldn't bring them home with us yet, but we had to meet them and the orphanage meet us before we could get the final approval.

Jerry could obviously tell something was bothering me. I hesitated telling him. That's why I was being so quiet. I didn't fully understand it myself.

"I have this overwhelming sense that their birth mom is an alcoholic, and she left them," I said. "I'm guessing that is why they ended up in an orphanage."

"That's strange," Jerry said.

"I know."

"You're probably just nervous."

I couldn't really explain it to him. The ominous feeling. I didn't know if it was discernment from the Holy Spirit or the enemy trying to ruin things for me by putting the thoughts in my head.

Maybe both?

Perhaps God was preparing me. I already knew that adopting these kids wasn't going to be easy. I'd already anticipated many of the problems and was willing to take them on. I realized that the kids could come with all kinds of behavioral problems as a result of their horrible upbringings.

I hadn't thought it might be alcoholism.

Was the enemy playing on my fears? Trying to make me as miserable as possible. Steal my joy. Even try to get me not to adopt the kids to circumvent God's will in the matter.

Jerry might be right. What if I was imagining it? I didn't really know that the mom was an alcoholic.

No. I was sure of it. God was telling me and I needed to listen.

But what did it mean?

I was prepared for almost anything. Not that. I'd dealt with so much alcoholism in my life with my mom and with Jerry, that I wasn't sure I could deal with that in the children. I'd tried so hard to keep it out of my life. The thought of bringing more alcohol problems into our home struck fear in me. I considered it one of my worst nightmares.

After everything I'd been through, why would I even want to do it?

The doubts were overwhelming me like a tsunami wave. As hard as I tried to tamp them down, I couldn't. No more than I could stop an actual wave of the ocean.

Didn't we have enough problems to deal with?

Caleb still had medical issues. Those would always be with us. Hurricane Katrina was still wreaking havoc in our lives. Things weren't back to normal at home and wouldn't be for a long time. If ever.

It also seemed like trouble kept coming into my life. One destructive wave after another.

Was I voluntarily bringing another storm into my house?

Jerry tried to be reassuring. "If that's the case, and their mother is an alcoholic" he said, "it'll be okay. You can relate to them. You'll be the perfect mom to kids who have an alcoholic mom."

He had a good point. If God was behind this adoption, then He'd have chosen me to be their mom for a reason. It seemed like that might be my calling in life. To deal with difficult children and circumstances.

If this was another test, I was certainly experienced in dealing with them. I would know what these kids had gone through. I knew what not to do. I wouldn't be the kind of mother my mom was to me. I'd love them like my own kids and would do anything for them. Jerry and I could give them a better life. They'd know God if they were with us.

Those thoughts didn't make it any easier. I was still afraid. It brought up so many of the feelings from my childhood that I'd tried to move beyond.

What if the kids grew up having problems with alcohol?

So many children of alcoholics had a problem with it later. I'd try to prevent it, but would I be able to?

"It would be just like God to give me two kids with issues I had in my past," I said to Jerry. Half sarcastically and half with trepidation.

Just talking about it was stirring up feelings from my childhood that I'd tried so hard to repress.

It wasn't too late to back out.

Even though it felt like it might be. We were on the plane. Heading to Romania. They were expecting us.

We'd also left Caleb behind which was something I swore I'd never do.

Could I back out? I didn't think so.

If I was flying the plane, I might've turned it around in the air and flown back home. I knew if we continued on, there'd be no turning back. Once I saw those kids, my heart would break for them, and I wouldn't be able to say no to being their mother.

Was I being silly?

We'd also gone to all this expense. What was I going to do? Tell Jerry and Carly that I didn't want to meet the kids? That we should go home as soon as we landed? They'd think I was crazy.

I felt trapped which only added to the anxiety. The entire flight I went back and forth between faith that things would be okay and worry that I was right, and I'd have to deal with alcoholism in these kids.

I just clammed up and didn't say much the rest of the flight. Kept those fears to myself.

We arrived at the orphanage. Tired but also filled with anticipation.

We were taken to a room to meet Denis and Diana.

They were so cute!

They warmed up quickly after opening some gifts. We took pictures with them and showed them their images on the camera display. They were fascinated. We put the camera around Denis's neck and let him take photographs.

His smile was so broad it filled his face and warmed my heart.

Carly went with us and fell in love with her sister immediately.

We were there for five days and spent several hours each day with the kids. They even allowed us to take Denis out of the orphanage to spend more time with him. We took him to an amusement park and out to eat.

On the last day, we had to say goodbye. I'll never forget the look in their eyes. Diana was sitting on my foot and clinging to my leg. The orphanage worker had to keep telling her we would be back to take them home forever.

By that point, I was fully on board. We were going to do anything we could to adopt those kids. It wouldn't be easy. There were still hurdles to overcome. A judge still had to sign off on it.

We might have to make several trips to Romania before we could actually bring the kids back with us. A lot could happen in that amount of time.

It broke my heart to leave them. We did our best to explain that we'd be back, but the disappointment was written all over their faces. As we drove away, Denis and Diana stood in the window. Diana was crying, and Denis slowly waved goodbye. Tears were streaming down his face as well.

There wasn't a dry eye in our car.

I had fallen in love with my kids. I say mine because that's what they were. From that day forward, they were my kids. Our kids. I knew it. God wanted us to adopt them. It was His will. To show His love, grace, and support to these precious children.

After three trips overseas and fully trusting God, we finally came home with a beautiful son who was seven and a daughter who was four.

Denis and Diana were officially adopted in July 2006 and became a part of the Roark family forever.

* * *

I wish I could say everything was peaches and cream and we all lived happily ever after. Like a fairy tale.

My life has never been that simple.

I've never doubted that God wanted us to adopt Denis and Diana. I have loved them like they were my own children. But my discernment had been right. They'd grown up with an alcoholic mother. God only knows what they had endured before we got them.

The first days of transition were a struggle which was to be expected. The kids didn't know English and that created immediate communication problems even though I was used to dealing with that. Caleb didn't speak either, but it was different having three children who couldn't communicate verbally.

Jerry's dad, Don, also passed away unexpectedly during that time, so we had that loss to deal with. The first thing we did when we brought Denis and Diana back to the States was to visit Gramps and Grammy's house.

Don and Floy bonded with the kids immediately. That's how they were. Wonderful and welcoming people. The kids loved them right away, so they felt the loss when Don died.

Both the kids struggled for years. We tried many counselors, but they were not trained in helping children with trauma and attachment issues. It felt like we were in a helpless situation, but we were not hopeless. My hope was in God, I had seen Him work so many times in the past. I was expecting God to help us, and He did. He directed our paths and opened doors many times.

Jerry and I were committed to praying daily that God would work in their hearts. He called us to obey and adopt our two kids, and we had to trust God to make the difference. We had to get out of God's way and fully give our concerns to Him.

Denis had to reach rock bottom before he'd reach out for help. I felt like he was running from God. Eventually, he left home and lived on the streets. We'd go months without hearing from him.

One day, he called out of the blue and asked if I could help him. He was tired of his life and needed help. I could tell he was serious this time.

"I've been praying daily for this moment to help you," I said. "I love you. Your dad loves you, and God loves you so much. We want you to find peace and the plan God has for your life."

I made a call to an Adult & Teen Challenge program. Our youngest daughter, Denis's biological sister, Diana, had completed a program at an Adult & Teen Challenge. She had her own issues as well. God had turned her life around. So much so, that she was offered an internship with the program and to this day is still using her life experiences to help others working for them.

A man from Teen Challenge called and let me know they had picked Denis up from the bus station and he was at their facility. I was relieved that he was finally off the streets. Later that first night, they allowed him to call me.

"Mom," Denis said, "thank you for not giving up on me and getting me some help."

"Denis," I said. "I'm so proud of you for making this decision. I love you! Everything is going to be okay."

Raising Denis and Diana was a challenging road, but God worked everything out.

We are so proud of both of our adoptive children. We cannot wait to see how God continues to use them for His glory.

Today both of my kids are doing well. I'm so proud of them for it.

* * *

Having five young kids in the household was challenging.

Thank God for baking. Some parents put their kids in front of the television set to distract them. Cooking had that effect on my kids. All of them loved to gather around me and help me bake.

Especially Caleb. Chocolate chip cookies were one of his favorites. They even became known as Caleb's Chocolate Chip cookies.

By having our freezer full of hundreds of cookie dough balls, it was easy to bake homemade cookies at a moment's notice. To stock the freezer, we made huge batches of cookie dough at one time. I would use a large ice cream scoop and scoop them out on a baking sheet lined with parchment paper. After a few hours in the freezer, I put them into freezer bags.

We were constantly baking. We loved sharing our cookies with others. Casey played baseball from age four through high school, plus middle school and high school football. We'd take cookies to the games and hand them out. Everyone helped, but Caleb was really into it.

He strutted around carrying bags of cookies even though he struggled to wedge them between his body and his cerebral palsy arm as he handed them out with his right hand. If anyone tried to help him, he'd quickly turn his body the opposite way. His cold shoulder said it all. He loved baking and sharing his goodies and seeing the joy it brought to others.

Casey's teammates would rave about Caleb's chocolate chip cookies. We surprised them with different candies in the cookies, including chopped holiday candies, candy bars, or M's & M's.

They made Caleb feel important. Seeing how others interacted with Caleb made my heart happy.

Here is the recipe:

Caleb's Chocolate Chip Cookies

4-1/2 cups all-purpose flour

1 teaspoon baking soda

1 teaspoon sea salt

1 tablespoon cornstarch

3/4 cup unsalted butter softened

3/4 cup shortening

2 cups packed dark brown sugar

1 cup sugar

1 1/2 TB pure vanilla

2 whole eggs

2 egg yolks

2-1/2 cups good quality semi-sweet chocolate chips

Sift together the flour, baking soda, salt, and cornstarch and set aside.

Using an electric mixer, cream together the soft butter and shortening

Mix in the granulated sugar and brown sugar until very creamy.

Add the eggs one at a time.

Mix in the pure vanilla.

Slowly add the dry ingredients. Do not overmix.

Mix the chocolate chips in by hand.

Use an ice cream scoop and drop cookies onto a baking sheet that has been lined with parchment paper.

Place the pan of cookie dough in the freezer at least 20 minutes before baking.

Bake in a preheated oven. Take the cookies out when they are just barely starting to turn brown.

Bake at 350 degrees for 24 minutes if using a 1/3 cup ice cream scoop.

Bake 20 minutes if using a regular size 1/4 cup ice cream scoop.

Try them. You'll love it.

CHAPTER TWENTY
NEW BEGINNINGS

Your attitude determines your direction.

Through each struggle in my life, God has been my last resort. I tried hard to handle things on my own before bringing them to Him. When I was at the end of my rope, I cried out to God and begged Him to help me.

If there's one message I want to convey through this memoir, it's that my approach was not the best one. God should be the first place I turn, not the last. I've suffered a lot of heartache over the years by not learning that lesson sooner.

This memoir wasn't meant to document all the bad things that have happened to me. My intention was not to chronicle all the ways in which others in my life have let me down. This book wasn't to highlight how their failures caused me pain.

Rather, the purpose of this book is to help you realize that God will help you through your struggles if you'll let Him. If He would help me, with all the mistakes I've made, He'll help anyone who is willing to ask Him for help.

Trust me. God can fix your problems faster than you can fix them on your own. At the very least, he'll give you the strength to get through them. Peace and joy in the midst of the trials which will produce the good work that Philippians 1:6 talks about.

This book has been cathartic from that standpoint. It's really helped to give me clarity. By writing my challenges down, I learned something else as well. I can now see clearly that God has not only been with me through the years but has blessed me as well. In ways I had never even realized.

I have so much to be thankful for. God has been so good to me.

Caleb, in spite of the challenges, has been one of the biggest blessings of my life. Jerry, despite the battles with alcoholism, has been a gift from God. I can't imagine going through life without him.

Hopefully, this book will remind you to remember the many ways God has blessed you. It sometimes doesn't feel like it in the midst of the trials. That's why you have to be reminded. That's why you have to look for the blessings. To recognize them. Sometimes, you don't see how God works all things together for good, (Romans 8:28), until years after the difficulties are over.

The Bible also says that trials produce wisdom. Wisdom is priceless. It comes from life lessons. James 1 says that God will give us wisdom if we ask. And he'll give it to us without judgment. In other words, God wants to give us wisdom, even if we got into the problems through our own foolishness.

God gives us small bits of it at a time for our brains to be able to comprehend it. It takes life's lessons balanced with God's Word to gain wisdom and understanding.

I think I've finally figured that out.

Do I do everything perfectly? No. Do I always respond in the right way to difficulties? No. But now I know what to do, and I rely on God a lot sooner than I used to.

Learning those truths doesn't mean the problems will end. It just gives you a way to deal with them. If you try to deal with them on your own, everyone and everything around you will suffer.

I tried to fix Jerry's problem with alcohol on my own. When did he finally overcome it? When I gave it over to God I began to thank Him for the miracle He was going to do in Jerry's life. That's when God had the freedom to begin to move.

I quit confronting Jerry about his problem. Stopped nagging him to get help. Those always ended in an argument anyway. My dad confronted my mom constantly which caused them to argue relentlessly and only made matters worse. It also caused Dad's blood pressure to always be out of control. High blood pressure led to his kidney failure and death at an early age.

My blood pressure was often out of control as well. I knew I had to do something before it was too late.

Giving it to God was the answer. Leaving Jerry wasn't an option. I would no more abandon Jerry to his problems than I would Denis and Diana to theirs. Or Caleb to his. It's not how I'm wired. I'm a fighter. God put these people in my life to be there for them. To help them through their difficulties. I firmly believe the marriage covenant between Jerry and me should last until death do us part.

It may have taken decades, but God was working on my heart during this time too. My lack of fully trusting God and extending forgiveness was delaying Jerry from being a recovering alcoholic. In some ways, what I was doing was worse.

After decades of Jerry's drinking, I had allowed bitterness to creep into my soul. I knew God forgave all my sins. I asked God to forgive me for taking matters into my own hands when He was not answering my prayers.

God was working on answering my prayers. If I believed He forgave me, I had to extend forgiveness to Jerry. It took me a while to get to this point because of the pain of growing up with an alcoholic.

I repented of all the anger. I made up my mind that each time I felt offended, I was going to forgive immediately. I didn't want to let unforgiveness or bitterness stew inside of me until I felt like exploding. I certainly didn't want my family and generations to come to be affected by my unforgiveness which gave me a bad attitude.

My heart's desire is for my family to see how much Jerry and I grew in our love for each other and our love for God during our difficult times.

* * *

I was doing better. We faced a number of trials and I responded better to them. I was stronger.

Then Covid hit.

Talk about testing your faith.

People were dying. The news made sure the numbers were in our face all the time. The country was facing one of its biggest challenges in decades.

I had a number of personal concerns as well.

Caleb.

With his health problems, he was at high risk if he got Covid. We couldn't risk him being around other people. Vacations were canceled, including our dream cruise to Alaska, and attending the K-love fan awards.

My fears were running rampant. What if Caleb had to go into the hospital? I couldn't be there with him. They weren't letting anyone inside. Not even to visit. Certainly not to spend the night.

Casey and Carly were in medical school and around Covid every day, so I couldn't see my other kids. I couldn't risk bringing Covid home to Caleb.

We couldn't go to church. Even doctor appointments were online.

Financial problems were a great worry as well. We had a rental property in Branson that provided us with income. All reservations were canceled, and it sat vacant for months.

The World Food Championships was canceled. The disappointment was overwhelming.

My social media presence was decimated. I had started a blog as a way of organizing my recipes. It grew to more than 570 recipes online and millions of people visited my website and Pinterest each year.

I was hacked four times. Each time, the hacker caused problems with my website. Eventually, they were able to wipe out everything. I've since learned that ISIS was behind it.

All my recipes, mailing list, and social media posts were all deleted. It would cost thousands of dollars and months of effort to duplicate the success. All my income was completely wiped out.

We were concerned about Jerry's job as well. A lot of companies were laying off salespeople. Jerry worked in the medical industry. Hospitals and medical offices didn't allow salespeople to come to their places of business. All major purchases were on hold anyway.

If he lost his job, we weren't sure what we'd do.

After a couple of months of crying, moping, and complaining about my blog being gone, and worrying about Jerry losing his job, I decided to spend a lot of time with God. A lot more than just reading the verse of the day or saying a couple of prayers. I began reading the Bible more than ever, keeping a prayer journal again, getting involved in a Bible class, and constantly asking God what His plans were for me.

I was learning to rely on God. Faster than I ever had before.

During this process, I kept thinking about Psalm 37:4 "Delight thyself also in the Lord: and he shall give thee the desires of thine heart." (KJV)

* * *

So here's what I decided to do.

1. Tune out all the news.

2. Focus on how faithful God has been in answering my prayers in the past. It's comforting to know that if He did it in the past, He can do it again.

3. Spend time reading old prayer journals.

4. Stop playing out all the worse-case scenarios in my head. I capture my negative thoughts and ask God to help me stop thinking about them. I put my trust in God to take care of what is worrying me.

5. Keep a prayer journal. Writing my prayers out to God has always helped me to release my worries to Him. A prayer journal gives me a feeling of peace. I'm putting my struggles in the hands of the only One who can do anything about them.

6. Start each day by spending time with God.

7. Thank God daily for answering my prayers even if He hasn't answered them yet. I want God to know I trust Him for what He's going to do during the challenging season.

8. Fall asleep each night listening to God's Word. I want it to be the last thing on my mind each day.

9. Listen to God's Word before getting out of bed each morning. I also ask God to use me each day to encourage others.

10. Focus on God and trust He is going to take care of me, allowing me to get through this horrible season our nation was facing.

It's made all the difference. It's given me a strategy for every difficult situation I might face in the future. I wished I'd learn these things sooner. I think I've finally turned the corner in the journey.

I've learned how to trust God in the difficult situations. I may not do it all perfectly, but God's grace will help me through it.

* * *

I've always wanted to write a book about my life's journey. I didn't want to forget where God helped me during some difficult and even traumatic times in my life. I wanted my kids and future grandkids to be encouraged to never give up and seek God with all their hearts.

I began writing this memoir to help me remember and see how God not only answered prayers but blew me away with His blessings.

As I penned these words, God did a tremendous work inside of me. He revealed areas where I needed to forgive others. If God forgave me for my sins, I needed to extend the forgiveness to others no matter what they have done to me. In doing so, I've found peace and even some understanding.

It also helped me to refocus on my baking career. After I lost my blog and all of my contacts, I felt helpless trying to start all over again. Writing about my times at the World Food Championships has energized me.

I've also always wanted to write cookbooks. I'm doing that now. They'll be released shortly after this memoir. I set goals to work on several cookbooks and share some of my life stories in each one.

As I did when blogging, I still have a dream that one day I can help moms with easy recipes allowing them to spend more time with their families around the table.

The benefits of eating with family around the table are endless. One of the best benefits is having a set time to communicate with each other. Having quick and easy meals has always helped me serve a meal to my family and enjoy talking to one another no matter what season of life.

My five kids are amazing, and I treasure all my time with them. I can't imagine my life without them. One of the greatest joys of my life is when we get to linger around the table after a meal. I now have two children with M.D.'s and a daughter-in-law with an M.D. I don't think it's solely because I made them do their homework, was a room mom, nor supported their school events.

These things are good to do, along with consistent prayers, but I'm convinced that having a routine of eating around the table played a heavy role in their higher education. Family dinner is a time to slow down, be present, and connect. It gives children a sense of belonging and teaches them they are a valuable part of the family.

Writing cookbooks is a way I can continue sharing my quick and easy recipes to encourage families to eat around the table.

I've started baking regularly again. I'm baking cakes for the Dream Center in Little Rock. They give children birthday cakes who might not otherwise receive one. Growing up, I had many birthdays without a cake. Baking birthday cakes is the perfect fit for me.

I'm also focused on improving my skills. I've been taking classes to improve my baking and cooking skills. I also want to become a better competitive baker. It's an excellent outlet for my competitive side and something I enjoy. The excitement of hearing my name called into the top ten each year at WFC overwhelms me with how good God is.

I know I can do all things through Christ, who gives me strength. I will continue learning and growing through my failures. Thank you for reading this far. I hope this book has been encouraging to you.

This is the final chapter of this book. However, the final chapter of my life has not been written. God has a lot more things in store for me in the future.

Here's one of them. Someday I'm going to win the dessert category and compete at the final table for The World Food Champion title.

I'll write about that in my next book.

Thanks again.

I love you all

Diane

Thank you for purchasing this memoir from best-selling author, Diane Roark. As an additional thank you, Diane would like to send you free gifts periodically.

If you'd like to receive:

Newsletters

Updates

New Releases

Announcements

Recipes

Sign up at:

https://wandering-butterfly-4036.ck.page/1d860b2617

Follow Diane at:

Facebook: https://www.facebook.com/recipesforourdailybread

Instagram: https://www.instagram.com/recipesforourbread/

ACKNOWLEDGMENTS

Blessed Beyond Words

I have many people to thank for your love and support over the years. It was a dream to use my life's hardships to encourage others, but I put it off. I didn't want to revisit all the difficult experiences. All I wanted to do was forget them and move on. After spending time with God and him nudging me to write about certain things, dealing with forgiveness and grace, this book was created.

The written stories were freeing. They were a reminder I was forgiven, and I had forgiven others. Therefore, the first person I most want to acknowledge is God. He helped me in the healing process while revisiting old wounds. He worked in me while writing my memoir, which I am forever grateful for.

Terry Toler. You are such a gifted writer and editor. Thank you for editing my memoir, coaching me, and for your publishing expertise which helped bring my story to print. I thank God you came into my life. You have been such a blessing.

Mike McCloud and World Food Championships staff and Competitors. Thank you for the opportunity to compete and be a part of the encouraging, supportive WFC FoodSport family. It has been a ride of which I am blessed to be a part. My foodie competitors/friends in-spire me to be the best I can be. Competing at WFC has taught me I am good enough. Feeling good enough is not only about being good enough to compete at WFC but feeling God's love and being good enough to be used by him despite all my weaknesses.

Show Hope staff who are always so encouraging and for your dili-gent work to help orphans get their forever homes. Thank you, espe-cially for your work in teaching and training parents, teachers, coun-selors, and others on how to love children with attachment disorders.

Mary Beth Chapman not only started Show Hope but inspired me to write this book after reading her story, *Choosing to See*. You and your sweet family, including Steven Curtis Chapman, are the real deal, com-passionate, loving, and serve others well. Thank you for being so en-couraging to me.

Life Groups at New Life Church. We have several groups, who have become family, including our families with special needs. Thank you to D'lisa and Matt Hass, Jimmy and Glenda Diamond, Cindy and Terry Viala, Susan and Randy Blue, Tracy and Marianne Shelton, and Chad and Kindall Denmon for leading us so well.

Landmark Church in Montgomery, Alabama. Your love, support, food, and prayers, during many of Caleb's difficult times, will never be forgotten. A special thank you to Melinda Hopson Rogers, (Craig Hopson who is with Jesus), Ramona Hopson, Mari Beth Moreland, Al Millergren, Tommy and Diane Patterson, Kay Randolph Bennett, Brenda and Sammy Smith, Dianne Mehaffey, Jimmy, and Vicki Nor-man, Donna Hopkins, Jeff and Ginny Langham, and the Blanchard family for providing us a place to stay in Atlanta.

Victoria Bordelon who has supported our family through every difficult adoption moment. Thank you for loving our family, praying, and understanding all our difficult times.

Aunt Bonnie and Debra. Your love and support helped me during those difficult childhood and teenage years. I am so grateful you were in my life.

Adult & Teen Challenge. Thank you for loving, supporting, and helping my adoptive children during some very challenging times.

Rick Warren's Daily Hope and Celebrate Recovery Program. There are no words for how grateful I am for your ministries. God used Celebrate Recovery to help change our family.

Conway Christian School and all Casey's coaches. Thank you for loving and pouring into him over the years.

Annie. Thank you for your Godly insight on so many things and baking with me at the World Food Championships. You are an amazingly talented cake artist. I am blessed to have you on my team and to have you as my friend.

Marsha. My Hero and Sister-In-Love. I know you don't like me saying you are my hero, but you are. Thank you for setting a positive example of how to go through physical and emotional heartache. Your pain has lasted over twenty years of fighting cancer three times and having chemo every three weeks. You are beautiful on the inside and out. You are always so encouraging. I am blessed to have you as my sister-in-law, friend, and sous chef at World Food Championships.

Donna (Daisy), Dale, and Danny. I love my siblings with all my heart! We have a bond that can't be broken. I could have never made it through a very difficult childhood without you being by my side. You are all so special to me beyond words. Thank you for always being so encouraging. I am so proud of how you have raised your children to be all they can be despite our childhood. You are always in my thoughts and prayers.

Jerry. The man of my dreams. I love watching you through the window in your office door as you spend time with God. You are such a wonderful example of God's goodness and the Godly man of my dreams. You are the most positive person I know, full of energy, laughter, and most importantly support. Thank you for encouraging me every day to go after my dreams. Thank you for putting up with me being excessively, compulsively, organizer, and sometimes demanding when practicing and preparing for WFC. I don't deserve your love and support. I love you with all my heart to death due us part.

Carly. You make me a better person and baker. My oldest thoughtful, intelligent child. I am so proud of you for going after, the dream God placed in your heart to be a pediatrician. You care deeply for your patients, and God uses you to bless them and their families. They are blessed to have you. Thank you for always making time for Caleb and treating him extremely special. Thank you for being my toughest critic when judging my food. I respect your opinion and know it helps me be a better cook, baker, and competitor. When you love my recipes, I am reassured that I have something special. Thank you for planning our vacations, being so thoughtful and my best friend.

Casey and Rachel. Thank you for the examples you set. God blessed us with two more medical doctors in the family. I am so proud and thankful you had each other during that stressful road. Thank you both for the example of putting God first in your life and in your marriage. Rachel, thank you for loving and encouraging my son. Casey, thank you for always being so calm and leading by example no matter how stressful the situation. Like your dad, you have taught me to laugh and enjoy life. Your crazy stunts make me smile. Your patients are blessed to have you both. They will never find more caring physicians. I cannot wait to see how God uses you to help others.

Caleb, My best friend. You are my brave and mighty warrior. You have been through so much pain with seventeen brain surgeries, cerebral palsy, and seizures. You have taught me to depend on God, call on

Him immediately, and trust Him with all my heart. I am thankful God gave me you as my full-time friend for the rest of our lives. You touch so many people with your strength and smiles. You also bless many people with your love of baking. Thank you for being my mixer operator and knowing exactly where everything is in the kitchen. Everyone needs a sous chef, and you are the best.

Diana. You were my little princess when your dad and I adopted you are you still are. You are beautiful on the inside and out. I am so proud of you for wanting to spend your life in full-time ministry helping others with similar struggles. You are full of joy, energy, and life. You set a wonderful example of God's love to everyone you meet. I cannot wait to see how God continues to use you to bless others.

Denis. I fell in love with you the day I met you. You are so smart, and I know God has great plans for your life. You have been through many heartaches but have overcome and come so far. Adopting you taught me how much God loves me and adopts us into His family. I cannot wait to see how God uses you for his glory.

Floy. Thank you for your continuous support. You are not just my mother-in-law but my friend. Words cannot thank you enough for all your endless help over the years. You are not only supportive but a Godly example to us all. Thank you for bringing up Jerry in the church and a Christian home filled with love. Thank you for being the best grammy. We are all blessed to have you in our lives.

And those of you who are reading this book. I'm so thankful for you choosing to read my story. You could have read any book, but you chose this one. I pray you and your families will be encouraged to seek God's will for your lives. He loves you and wants the very best for each one of you.

In Memory of:

Carl Hill. My Daddy, I Miss You Every Day! I am the person I am today because of your love and support. Thank you for never leaving me. I love and miss you with all my heart every day.

Don Roark. The best Father-In-Love. Thank you for being the best Father-in-Law I could ever have. I am beyond blessed to have had your endless help, encouragement, and support. I love and miss you so much!

Doris Gatlin, and Dorothy Brooks. I could not have asked for better aunts. Your love and support helped me during those difficult childhood and teenage years. I am so grateful you were in my life.

ABOUT THE AUTHOR

Diane Roark is an annual competitor at the World Food Championships with four top five finishes and two rare perfect scores. She's a best-selling author, blogger, and mother of five adult children. She lives in Arkansas with her husband of thirty-eight years.

Diane can be followed at:
Facebook: https://www.facebook.com/recipesforourdailybread
Instagram: https://www.instagram.com/recipesforourbread/

Reviews are gold to authors!
If you've enjoyed this book, would you consider rating it
and reviewing it
https://www.amazon.com/author/recipesfordailybread.

A portion of proceeds goes to charities.

www.ingramcontent.com/pod-product-compliance
Lightning Source LLC
Chambersburg PA
CBHW020443130626
46549CB00001B/285